THE WORKING LIFE

A Worker on the Transcontinental Railroad

JAMES BARTER

LUCENT BOOKS®

THOMSON
™
GALE

San Diego • Detroit • New York • San Francisco • Cleveland • New Haven, Conn. • Waterville, Maine • London • Munich

On cover: Like their counterparts in the mid-nineteenth century, this 1944 Nevada railroad crew lays track.

LIBRARY OF CONGRESS CATALOGING-IN-PUBLICATION DATA

Barter, James
    A worker on the transcontinental railroad / by James Barter.
        v. cm. — (The working life series)
Contents: Brain power in muddy boots—A day on the construction line—The ordeal of camp life—Extreme dangers—Diversions from agonizing work—The exotic and secretive world of the Chinese.
    ISBN 1-59018-247-2 (hardback : alk. paper)
    1. Railroad construction workers—United States—History—19th century—Juvenile literature. 2. Railroads—United States—History—19th century—Juvenile literature. [1. Railroad construction workers—History—19th century. 2. Railroads—History.] I. Title. II. Series.
    HD8039.R3152.U5378 2003
    331.7'61385'097309034—dc21

                                                                    2002009883

Printed in the United States of America

CONTENTS

FOREWORD

"The strongest bond of human sympathy outside the family relations should be one uniting all working people of all nations and tongues and kindreds."

Abraham Lincoln, 1864

Work is a common activity in which almost all people engage. It is probably the most universal of human experiences, the drive to work. As Henry Ford, inventor of the Model T said, "There will never be a system invented which will do away with the necessity of work." For many people, work takes up most of their day. They spend more time with their coworkers than family and friends. And the common goals people pursue on the job may be among the first thoughts that they have in the morning, and the last that they may have at night.

While the idea of work is universal, the way it is done and who performs it varies considerably throughout history. The story of work is inextricably tied to the history of technology, the history of culture, and the history of gender and race. When the typewriter was invented, for example, it was considered the exclusive domain of men who worked as secretaries. As women workers became more accepted, the secretarial role was gradually filled by women. Finally, with the invention of the computer, the modern secretary spends little time actually typing correspondence. Files are delivered via computer, and more time is spent on other tasks than the manual typing of correspondence and business.

This is just one example of how work brings together technology, gender, and culture. Another example is the American plantation slave. The harvesting of cotton was initially so cumbersome and time-consuming that even with slaves, its profitability was doubtful. With the invention of the cotton gin, however, efficiency improved, and slavery became a viable agricultural tool. It also became a Southern tradition and institution, enough that the South was willing to go to war to preserve it.

The books in Lucent's Working Life series strive to show the intermingling of work, and its reflection in culture, technology, race, and gender. Indeed, history viewed through the perspective of the average worker is both enlightening and fascinating. Take the history of the typewriter, mentioned above. Readers today have access to more technology than any of their historical counterparts, and, in fact, though they would find the typewriter's keyboard familiar, they would find using it a bore. Finding out that people spent their days sitting over that machine (with no talk of carpal tunnel syndrome!) and were valued if they made no typing errors because corrections were cumbersome to make and, in some legal professions, made documents invalid, is an interesting story that involves many different aspects of history.

The desire to work is almost innate. As German socialist Ferdinand Lassalle said in the 1850s, "Workingmen we all are so far as we have the desire to make ourselves useful to human society in any way whatever." Yet each historical period offers a million different stories of the history of each job and how it was performed. And that history is the history of human society.

Each book in the Working Life series strives to tell the tale of these anonymous workers. Primary source quotes offer veracity and immediacy to each volume, letting the workers themselves tell their stories. In addition, thorough bibliographies tell students where they can find out more information and complete indexes allow for easy perusal of the text. While students learn about the work of years gone by, they gain empathy for those who toil, and, perhaps, a universal pride in taking up the work that will someday be theirs.

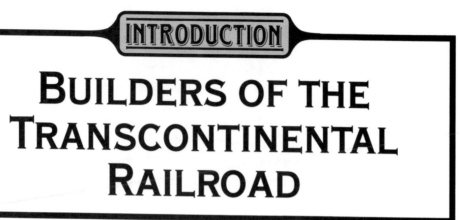

INTRODUCTION

BUILDERS OF THE TRANSCONTINENTAL RAILROAD

American historians recording the linking of the East Coast with the West Coast by the transcontinental railroad have uniformly focused on two principal themes: the importance of a handful of prominent men who led the Herculean effort and the actual physical construction involved with the laying of the rails. These historical writings, both scholarly and popular, paint an impressive picture of this epic event by blending the superlative achievements of this small group of celebrated men among statistical reports documenting sums of money spent, tonnage of steel shipped, miles of track spiked, barrels of blasting powder detonated, and seemingly insurmountable obstacles that were conquered along the wearisome path.

A notable gap in the historical record of this event is a glimpse into the working lives of the crew mem-

bers. These were the men who performed the actual physical construction: the surveyors of the route, the blasters of the tunnels, the builders of the bridges, and the pounders of the iron railroad spikes. When President Abraham Lincoln pushed forward with the decision to build the railroad that would connect California with the rest of the nation, his advisers knew that it would be the longest railroad in the world, running between the two terminus cities of Council Bluffs, Iowa, the most western extent of America's railroad in 1860, and Sacramento, California.

Lincoln's advisers also knew that such a formidable enterprise would require thousands of men performing dozens of different tasks under challenging conditions. To speed the project, Congress passed the Railroad Act of 1862 authorizing one railroad company to start at each terminus and to work toward the other. The Union Pacific Railroad began at Council Bluffs working west across the relatively flat and desolate Great Plains, while the Central Pacific Railroad began at Sacramento moving east up and over the rugged Sierra Nevada mountain range. As the two railroads pushed out into the wilderness of America's Great Plains, thousands of nameless able-bodied men were hired to roll up their sleeves and perform the thankless, grueling work on what many historians consider America's greatest engineering endeavor of its time.

It is not surprising that these common workers have been lost in the flurry of the excitement surrounding this heroic event. The vast majority of the men, estimated to have run as high as 90 percent, were poor, illiterate immigrants who had few options other than to accept the hard menial railroad work that most Americans refused. Of the estimated twenty to twenty-five thousand immigrants who worked on the rails, most of those employed by the Central Pacific Railroad arrived from China, and most of those employed by the Union Pacific Railroad came from Europe, principally from Ireland. The Chinese and Irish had come from opposite hemispheres and from seemingly opposite cultures, yet all

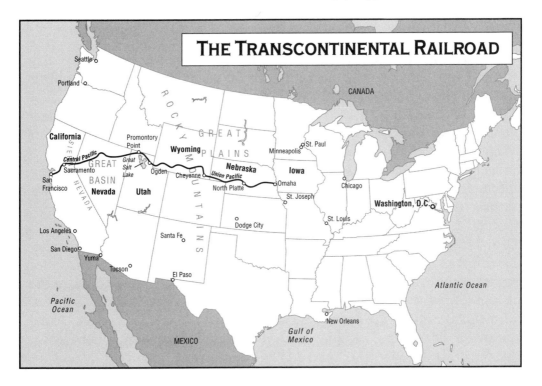

THE TRANSCONTINENTAL RAILROAD

*Connecting California to the rest of the country by rail was an immense engineering feat.
An illustration records the venture's successful outcome.*

sought out America with the hope of escaping the poverty within their own countries in favor of more optimistic futures in their new land.

Uneducated, far from home, and moving a mile or two each day down the seemingly endless, desolate line, pitifully few laborers wrote letters or journals that have survived to remind us of their experiences and indomitable spirits. As a result of this unfortunate lack of documentation, most of what historians know about the building of the transcontinental railroad comes from the pens of the educated and better-paid employees. These were the men who worked among the upper echelon of construction engineers, crew managers, owners, and financiers who thoroughly documented the progress of the railroad—but not the lives of the men building it.

The British journalist and explorer Henry Morton Stanley traveled across America and wrote newspaper articles about the construction of the transcontinental railroad. He understood that the labor of the nameless mass of crew members would quickly be forgotten:

Step by step towards the Occident [west] he throws the earth into a straight line over which will be placed the iron rails for the million travelers who will roll by without a thought to the navvies [grunt workers] who toiled for them. The Irishman heaves his spade full on the common heap, smokes his dundee [clay pipe], and, eats his cooked rations at the "shebang" [any shabby place], has his petty quarrels, is reckless of the future, sanguine of the present, toils out his carol day by day.[1]

The workers' story is a fascinating component of the history of the construction of the railroad. By sifting through newspaper articles, a few key journals, offhanded comments by managers about the men, historical photographs, private correspondences, congressional testimony, and historical odds and ends, a picture of the workers begins to emerge. After 130 years of documenting the achievements of a few celebrated railroad tycoons, the time is long overdue to honor and to tell the story of the thousands of men who performed the day-to-day backbreaking labor that bound the nation with an eighteen-hundred-mile steel band from Iowa to California.

CHAPTER 1

GETTING ORGANIZED

The moment Congress passed the Railroad Act authorizing the construction of the transcontinental railroad, the financiers and members of the boards of directors for the two chosen railroads set to work organizing the thousands of intricate tasks needed to ensure the success of this unprecedented endeavor.

The magnitude and importance of linking the West Coast with the rest of the nation was understood by America's political, military, and industrial leaders and was articulated in 1858 by one of America's leading railroad men, Henry Poor, editor of *Poor's Manual of Railroads of the United States,* who wrote: "In a railroad to the Pacific we have a great national work, transcending in its magnitude, and in its results, anything yet attempted by man. By its execution, we are to accomplish our appropriate mission, [linking the country] and a

greater one than any yet fulfilled by any nation."[2]

The meaning of the project was also keenly understood by both railroad companies. Each would receive from the federal government sixteen thousand dollars for every mile of track completed on flat terrain and forty-eight thousand dollars for each mile completed over the mountains. In addition to the money, the government also agreed to give each company 12,800 acres—twenty square miles—of federal land for each mile of track laid.

Each railroad had its own unique set of priorities that had to be addressed before the first mile of rail could be spiked. Senior managers of each company, many of whom had experience building railroads along the East Coast, needed to address a seemingly endless list of logistical nightmares before they could expect to see their first dime or acre of land from the government.

OBSTACLES IN THE PATH OF THE RAILS

The directors of both railroads understood that many obstacles lay in the path of the rails. Both companies knew the work would be long, tedious, and costly in terms of men and money. Some were not even certain that the transcontinental railroad could be built. No one summed up this sense of trepidation and uncertainty more

Collis Huntington was not confident that carving the railroad's path through the rugged Sierra Nevada mountains was possible.

clearly than Collis Huntington, one of the four owners of the Central Pacific, who made the following comment during the groundbreaking ceremony for the Central Pacific:

> If you want to jubilate over driving the first spike, go ahead and do it. I don't. Those mountains over there [the Sierras] look too ugly and I see too much work ahead of us. We may fail, and if we do, I want to have as few people know it as we can. And if we get up a jubilation, everybody will remember it. Anybody can drive the first spike, but there are many months of labor and unrest between the first and last spike.[3]

As Huntington indicated in his speech, the Central Pacific worried most of all about conquering the Sierra Nevada mountain range that stood in the path of their railroad along the border shared by California and Nevada. Although the summit of the Sierras was only a little more than one hundred miles from the starting point in Sacramento, its ten-thousand-foot rugged peaks created a formidable barrier to steel rails that would need to go up steep switchback grades, across bridges spanning deep gorges with swollen rivers, and through numerous tunnels blasted through granite mountains. The directors knew that the problem of conquering the Sierras

A Union Pacific construction crew takes a break. Such workers endured backbreaking physical labor, brutal weather, and danger from Indian attacks.

would be further complicated by the region's notorious snowstorms which, when combined with the treacherous terrain, were known to be a death trap to many early travelers who foolishly dared to traverse them.

In addition to the Sierras, the Central Pacific worried about solving several colossal logistical problems. First on the list was finding adequate manpower along the West Coast to build over the Sierras. Most Californians in 1862 capable of hard physical labor were miners who preferred to take their chances in the goldfields rather than face the punishing work of constructing a railroad. Although thousands of Chinese men toiling in mines might be available to help lay the rails, the directors of the railroad did not believe they were strong enough or skilled enough to be of assistance.

The situation for the Union Pacific Railroad was also bleak. The major obstacle for their crews moving west from Iowa across the Great Plains was the possibility of attacks by numerous Indian tribes that had lived in this large expanse for thousands of years. Long before 1862, wagon trains had been ambushed and the pioneers killed on their way west to California and Oregon. Knowing that the Indians would resist the railroad workers, legislators passed the Railroad Act, which provided that the government, "Shall extinguish as rapidly as possible the Indian titles to all lands falling under the operation of this act."[4] Nonetheless, the prospect of laying rails while fighting Indians was daunting.

The Union Pacific also had its share of logistical nightmares. Working west across the dry, open plains meant many natural resources would be in short supply. Plentiful supplies of timber needed for the millions of ties that would be set and for the heavy beams to construct bridges were a rare resource. Then there was the problem of finding sufficient water supplies in the hot territories of present-day Nebraska, Wyoming, and Utah that were needed for the men, horses, and steam-driven locomotives. Henry Poor traversed the terrain and then published this dreary description of the terrain in a railroad magazine: "Through an uninhabited, and, for the greater part, we may say an uninhabitable country, nearly destitute of wood, extensive districts of it destitute of water; over mountain ranges whose summits are white with eternal snows; over deserts parched under an unclouded sky."[5]

Finally, thousands of men would be needed at a time when the Civil War still dragged on. Most young men capable of performing hard labor were fighting in either the Union or Confederate army.

Neither the Union Pacific nor the Central Pacific was prepared to start the actual construction. Fortunately for both railroad companies, however, plenty of preliminary work needed to be completed before spiking rails, blasting through tunnels, or constructing bridges. Both railroads started by hiring teams of senior construction personnel to organize and supervise a myriad of construction decisions that needed resolution before the rail crews could begin the actual work of laying track.

HIRING SENIOR CONSTRUCTION PERSONNEL

Refusing to allow the war to derail the transcontinental railroad, company owners pushed forward with the job of finding and hiring on-site management teams smart enough and tough enough to impose their will on the many work crews that would soon be needed to build the railroad. Controlling, directing, and motivating men making little money in exchange for brutally hard work required masterful yet uncompromising management skills.

❧ MANAGEMENT STYLES ON THE RAILROAD ❧

Successfully managing work crews required more than standing six feet tall with an intimidating physique. Crew bosses had to have an iron demeanor as well. According to American historian David Howard Bain in his book the *Empire Express,* Strobridge, unlike Crocker or the Casement brothers, was "A pure fire breather with a demon's temper, asbestos lungs, and the sharpest, most profane tongue in the state, he used physical fear as his prime managerial tool."

Crocker, on the other hand, although capable of wielding his bullwhip, saw himself as possessing a management style based on respect. He attributed his successful management style to his younger days when he learned the importance of gaining the respect of the crews, not by frightening them, but rather by working right along with them. David Howard Bain quotes Crocker in *Empire Ex-press* as saying, "I had worked them in the ore-beds, and in the coal pits, and worked them all sorts of ways, and had worked myself right along with them. I knew how to manage men."

Strobridge, who was known to beat men with his fists, swing at them with a pick handle, and verbally abuse them, drew criticism from Crocker because of his meanness. David Howard Bain reports that Crocker once criticized Strobridge saying to him, "Don't talk so to the men—they are human creatures—don't talk so roughly to them." To this rebuff Strobridge replied, "You have *got* to do it, and *you* will come to it; you cannot talk to them as though you were talking to gentlemen, because they are not gentlemen. They are about as near brutes as they can get."

Crocker later grudgingly admitted that Strobridge was probably correct.

Highest on the list of managers were construction superintendents, one for each railroad company. The construction superintendents were the highest ranking managers actually working in the construction camps and each was vested with final authority over all construction decisions and all employees. The Central Pacific Railroad chose as their construction superintendent Jim Strobridge and the Union Pacific hired John Casement. Both men had built railroads prior to serving in the Civil War. The men also had reputations as fearless leaders, which they had proven as officers. Each was capable of publicly disciplining his men in a brutal and often bloody manner as a deterrent to others who might refuse orders or challenge authority.

THE ONE-EYED BOSS MAN

Jim Strobridge was willing to work for $125 a month. "Stro," as his men called him, pushed men to do their work by sheer strength of his bull-headed personality that was backed up by an equally fear-inspiring physical appearance. An Irishman over six feet tall, Strobridge towered above nearly everyone, and his rugged face and barrel-chested torso made most men reluctant to challenge his authority.

Strobridge projected an intimidating mystique that stemmed from the black patch he wore over one eye socket. He had lost the eye in a blasting accident while working in a mine. Rumors of the incident claimed that he entered a tunnel after a blast, unaware that one of the long fuses leading to a charge was still burning. When the powder blew, a piece of granite embedded in his eye. His legend for toughness was born the moment he allegedly pulled the granite chip from his bleeding eye and continued barking orders. His appearance later earned him the nickname among the Chinese as the "one-eyed boss man."

If Strobridge's powerful physique and eye patch were not enough to identify him as the man in charge, the pick handle he carried to settle disputes among his men was decisive. Such an intimidating presence prompted American historian David Howard Bain to portray Strobridge as, "A pure fire-breather with a demon's temper, asbestos lungs, and

❧ THE PRIVATE LIFE ❧ OF THE SUPERINTENDENT

The camp superintendents received certain privileges afforded no other workers on the railroad. One such privilege was the railroad car that was the private home for the superintendent. On the Central Pacific, superintendent Strobridge shared the car with his wife, the only woman in camp. On January 11, 1869, a newspaper reporter for the Vallejo Evening Chronicle *was invited to have a look at this car and he described it in the following detail:*

In the forward car is Mr. Strobridge's residence and office. It is neatly fitted up and well furnished, and an awning veranda, with a canary bird swinging at the front door, gives it a home-like appearance. Here Mr. Strobridge spends his time with his family and receives visitors. A battery is on the car, and an operator to work it.

the sharpest, most profane tongue in the state, he used physical fear as his prime management tool."[6]

MANAGEMENT BY BULLWHIP

John Casement also had a track record of driving his men relentlessly. Casement had the intimidating physique of a lumberjack and regularly carried a .44 pistol strapped to his waist and a bullwhip in his hand, both of which he used. When he walked among his troops dragging his bullwhip, everyone understood his management style and either got out of his way or unflinchingly carried out his orders.

The first job for both construction superintendents was to hire the men who could provide the brainpower needed to solve all of the engineering and mathematical problems. Such men were the topographical engineers responsible for selecting the most expeditious route for each company's track, the surveyors needed to determine the precise positioning of the track, and a collection of mathematicians and engineers to perform calculations for track inclines and curves, tunnel placement and shape, and the construction of an array of bridges.

TOPOGRAPHICAL ENGINEERS— ROUGHING OUT THE ROUTE

No one person or group had yet determined the path of the transcontinental railroad. Until that happened, not a single tie could be set, not a single rail spiked, not a bridge constructed. The teams of topographical engineers, known as "topogs," climbed mountains and forded rivers to map the best route for the rails.

Selecting the right course was a critical undertaking. The job of the topographical engineers was twofold: First, locate a path that would support the construction crews with water for the men, horses, and the steam locomotives, and with lumber for millions of ties and dozens of bridges. Second, locate the simplest, most direct route possible. This meant complying with the requirements in the Railroad Act such as avoiding grades steeper than one hundred feet per mile and permitting no curves tighter than ten degrees. Also of critical importance were locating the shortest route between towns, bridging rivers at the narrowest points, selecting solid geologic foundations capable of supporting the weight of a train, locating the lowest passes through mountain ranges, and avoiding the need for tunnels.

To locate and map the most expeditious routes, engineers had to forsake their homes in big cities to explore unmapped territory. Working in temporary shacks and on the backs of mules in the mountains and deserts, they worked late into the night under adverse conditions. One

Topographical engineers faced the daunting task of selecting the most direct route for the railway.

of the more poetic descriptions of this work was that of reporter Bert Richardson. While traveling in the Sierras he wrote:

> The floor was covered with maps, profiles, and diagrams, held down at the corners by candlesticks to keep them from rolling up. On their knees were superintendents, directors, and surveyors, creeping from one map to another, and earnestly discussing the plans of their magnificent enterprise. Outside, the night wind moaned and shrieked.[7]

As the Union Pacific's topographical engineers pushed west across the Great Plains deep into the domain of hostile Native American tribes, conflict arose. Tribes were protecting their homes from invasion, while the railroad recognized no tribal rights to the land. As far as the railroad was concerned, it was their land. Engineer James Evans describes these conflicts in a characteristically insensitive way:

> The hostility of the Indians makes explorations extremely difficult and dangerous. Until they are exterminated, or so far reduced in numbers as to make their power contemptible, no safety will be found in that vast district extending from Fort Kearney to the mountains, and beyond.[8]

Indian attacks demanded more of these men than filing engineering reports and maps. In addition to their technical responsibilities, the engineering teams of the Union Pacific eventually were required to carry rifles. Head engineer, Major General Grenville M. Dodge, disclosed in his book *How We Built the Union Pacific Railway* the dangers encountered by his topographical crews:

Head engineer Grenville M. Dodge and his topographical teams traveled with armed escorts.

> Each party would thus consist of from eighteen to twenty-two men, all armed. Each party entering a country occupied by hostile Indians was generally furnished with a military escort of ten men to accompany under a competent officer. Notwithstanding this protection, the parties are often attacked, their chief, or some of their men killed or wounded, and their stock run off.[9]

Regardless of dangers, the engineers provided remarkably detailed reports. Union Pacific engineer, General William J. Palmer, chose what he believed to be the best place to bridge a river by describing the fording location with this detailed profile: "The river is 12 feet deep, when low, 300–400 feet wide, and rises 21 feet in summer, from the melting of snow. Well graveled on either bank, this is a favorable point for the departure of the line westwardly across the Great Basin."[10]

Deprivation was also part of the job description of the topographical engineers. The hardworking Theodore D. Judah, who provided the initial topographical report for the Central Pacific Railroad, spent months hiking and riding the back of a mule through the rugged Sierras searching

Topographical engineer Theodore D. Judah spent months exploring the Sierras.

for the best route over this alpine terrain. He crossed the crest of the Sierra twenty-three times before selecting the most reliable route. Letters to his wife detailed the deprivation he experienced sleeping in a bedroll, scavenging for food, and in the winter burrowing beneath tree roots to escape frostbite: "I have been fearful of removing my soaking boots because the swelling of my feet may prevent me from getting them back on. I have not been able to move the toes on my right foot today and fear I may need to amputate them if I don't get down [out of the Sierras] soon."[11]

When a young engineer working alongside Judah arrived in camp, he was assigned a corner of a tent where he was to sleep. Recalling his first night, he wrote home that someone "gave me a small hand ax and went with me to find a small fir tree from which to cut boughs to make a mattress for my bed. The ends of the boughs I stuck into the ground, laid my canvas on them, then my blankets, and used my backpack for a pillow."[12]

SURVEYORS— SPYING OUT A LINE

Working in teams of ten to fifteen men, the surveying crews followed the route specified by the topographical engineers. Their job was to specify the precise location for the rails, referred to as "spying out a line." With maps in hand and using transits, telescope-like instruments capable of accurately measuring long distances, elevations, and angles, surveyors applied many principles of geometry for determining elevations, curves, and distances between two points. As the teams progressed they placed markers of various types, indicating to the rail crews who would later follow where to grade the roadbed, cut tunnels, and build bridges.

The markers they used depended upon the terrain and density of brush, trees, and boulders. The most common types were long ropes strung from tree to tree, heavily painted red chalk lines, wood stakes marked in pencil with instructions, and occasionally bottles turned upside down with notes inside specifying technical directions. Historian Stephen E. Ambrose states in his book, *Nothing Like It in the World: The Men Who Built the Transcontinental Railroad 1863–1869,* that the markers indicated the bed that the track would follow: "Sometimes it was flat; sometimes it crossed ridges that would have to be cut; sometimes there were drainage ditches that must be filled, or occasionally creeks that must be bridged."[13]

❧ LONG DAYS FOR SURVEYORS ❧

Many of the men performing the hard physical labor of splitting rock and setting rails often had the misconception that the work performed by the surveyors and topographical engineers was easy mental work. Nothing could have been further from the truth. When Theodore D. Judah and his crew carried out their initial survey of the Sierra mountain range they camped in tents every night even when the temperatures plunged below freezing, chipped ice in order to drink water, and put up with unbelievable inconveniences while traversing the mountains. The following excerpt from one of Judah's letters to his wife, found in historian David Howard Bain's book Empire Express, *attests to the difficulties:*

There are ten men in my party. And I am running a line through the most difficult country ever conceived of for a Rail Road. And had no time to explore it in advance. I get my breakfast and am off by sunrise every morning, and in the saddle all day long over hills mountains ravines & etc. And come home tired out. Then in the evening I have foreman at work till after ten PM plotting up work— and it gives me no time to come down. . . . Some time we will come out on horseback over this country together and you shall see what I have been doing.

Surveyors working in the Sierras faced extremely hazardous conditions.

Spying out a line had its dangers. It was not simply a matter of setting up markers. Indian attacks against Union Pacific surveyors caused some to desert. As head surveyor Samuel Reed wrote in 1866, the grading was "not as well advanced as it should be. The Indian scene and severe storms has drove most of the men off the line."[14]

Surveyors in the Sierras faced other dangers. Each man was issued a pair of hobnailed boots with heels that had short steel spikes to dig into the dirt, leaves, and fallen pine needles. These boots prevented men from slip-ping down sheer cliffs and provided excellent traction on fallen trees often used to ford rivers and streams. Each surveyor was also issued a large hand ax to hack his way through densely forested terrain. As one young surveyor wrote home, "We had not gone more than 1000 feet when the line struck a big pine, which meant it must come down, and it was here that the axes came in handy. After two hours work the giant fell, which meant another turn at the grindstone the next morning."[15]

The completion of all topographical maps and the placement of railbed markers ended the first phase of the construction process and set the stage for the start of the second stage: laying the rails. Construction superintendents for both railroads now began hiring the thousands of unskilled workers needed to perform the hard manual labor on the work gangs. A logistical effort of this magnitude first required finding and hiring enough men, but it also required setting up camps where the men would be organized into work crews and where they would live as each railroad moved beyond America's towns and cities into the wilderness.

CHAPTER 2

CAMP LIFE ON THE CENTRAL PACIFIC

Strobridge understood that gathering thousands of men and horses amid mountains of supplies and construction materials required a site where all elements could be assembled, organized, and effectively put to work. Such a site would have to support a small city, catering to the many personal needs of the men while solving all logistical problems associated with supplying tons of steel and lumber along with the tools and horses to do the job.

Construction trains served as mobile support headquarters for the rail workers.

On a railroad project constantly on the move, the only effective site would be one capable of moving along with the men. To accomplish such an atypical organizational feat, a temporary mobile site, known to the men as simply "the camp," was designed that consisted of horse-drawn wagons and railroad cars that functioned as mobile offices, stores, kitchens, repair shops, first-aid stations, and sleeping accommodations.

Before the railroad departed Sacramento, the mobile camp needed to be stocked with everything required for crossing the cold, treacherous peaks of the Sierras and then later restocked to handle the hot flat deserts of Nevada and Utah until it joined the Union Pacific. The two geographies could hardly have been more different. While the mobile camp was being stockpiled, Strobridge tackled the problem of finding and hiring enough men to get construction underway.

HIRING THE RAIL CREWS

The start of the actual construction on the Central Pacific began when two leaders of the Central Pacific, construction superintendent Jim Strobridge and Charles Crocker, the only owner willing to appear on-site and help supervise the effort, posted advertisements in several California newspapers in January 1863 offering long-term employment for five thousand men with a guaranteed wage of "$30 a month plus meals for strong able-bodied men for constant and permanent work."[16] No other personal qualities or work experience was specified in the advertisements —anyone showing up would be hired.

The Central Pacific was hoping to attract gold miners whose luck had run out working claims that had failed to produce gold. Thousands of such men wandered the foothills. When only about six hundred men responded, Strobridge knew he had problems. Crocker chimed in, noting that gold fever continued to pulse through the veins of the few miners they did hire: "Most of the men working on the road were merely working for a stake [money]. When they got that, they would go off to the mines, and we could not hold them, except in rare instances, more than a very little while."[17]

Failing to attract enough workers, Central Pacific management reluctantly appealed to the estimated sixty thousand Chinese workers living in northern California. Strobridge, who did not believe the Chinese were physically strong enough to perform the hard work, commented, "They are too delicate. They have too small hands."[18] Nonetheless, he was forced to give them a chance. Paying them twenty-four dollars a month without meals, they were making about half what their white counterparts made. In spite of the discrepancy, they signed up and worked hard. In March 1866 the *Placerville Herald* newspaper published this statement indicating that many Chinese were working and that all who applied would be hired:

> As the favorable season for grading is being entered upon, the company [Central Pacific] is increasing their force of laborers, who are distributed at new camps above Dutch Flat. Large numbers of Chinamen have been taking that direction of late, and it is understood that all who choose to go can find employment.[19]

What had occurred over a fairly short period was revolutionary for its time. The composition of the Central Pacific labor force became increasingly Chinese until they claimed 90 percent of all work assignments. In a short time their numbers dominated the crew, giving the entire camp a distinctive Chinese character.

THE EXOTIC AND SECRETIVE WORLD OF THE CHINESE

The Chinese workers on the Central Pacific railroad were a source of contradiction to everyone who saw them. They evoked racial resentment, yet at

Although Chinese workers were subjected to racism, they were also a source of fascination to whites.

the same time, fascination among white railroad workers as well as in the general citizenry of America. Historian Robert West Howard cites an Irish crew member who admitted, "To the Irish, the Chinese look strange, with their blue cotton pants flopping, dishpan-shaped hats shadowing grave faces, [and] delicate hands hidden in billowing sleeves."[20] Newspaper reporters representing dozens of papers loved to visit their camps, observe their unique style of work, their social activities, and write stories about their exotic customs as well as the significant contribution they were making on the transcontinental railroad.

Virtually all historical sources that addressed the Chinese and their role in building the railroad emphasized their cultural differences and described their intentions to sustain a substantial part of their Chinese culture rather than dilute it with the culture of white Californians. In this regard, few Chinese learned the English language, bought Western clothing, adopted Western hairstyles, or changed their eating habits to coincide with the other railroad workers.

The single factor that historians believe accounted for this unusual phenomenon was the isolation that most Chinese experienced throughout California when they arrived to work in the goldfields. According to historian Robert F.G. Spier, "It is altogether probable that some longtime Chinese residents of America never spoke to a native American, nor entered his home or place of business."[21]

Besides the easily observable cultural differences were a few that were not so obvious, yet significant. One was the value expressed by the Chinese that their toil had a long-term purpose. The Chinese workers saved a large percent of their monthly salary for use when the railroad job was completed. Unlike the vast majority of white workers who had little to show for their effort when the transcontinental railroad was completed, most Chinese had saved enough money to purchase businesses, land, and homes either in China or America.

TONG ORGANIZATIONS

One of the reasons the Chinese were so successful is that they understood the value of organization. Unlike the white crew members who embraced the value of the individual worker, the Chinese embraced the value of the group. As the thousands of Chinese workers arrived in railroad camps high up in the Sierras, they immediately joined one of six associations, called "Tongs," if they had not already done so before arriving.

The six Tongs, also referred to as the "Six Companies," were benevolent organizations principally concerned for the well-being of their members. Although their origins were rooted in secret and sometimes crimi-

❧ TONG WARS ❧

Neither white workers nor their managers gained much insight into the closed Chinese society within the camps. Preferring to live isolated from the white workers, the Chinese regulated themselves and resolved their own disputes internally rather than allowing railroad managers in to resolve them. As far as the railroad managers were concerned, they were perfectly happy to allow the Chinese to maintain their own independence—up to a point.

Money was involved in the memberships within the six Tong companies and, from time to time, disputes arose, even over small amounts. Occasional small feuds between the Tongs erupted in the railroad camps, but quick internal resolutions obviated the need for outside management intervention. The policy of the Central Pacific managers was to allow the Chinese to resolve their own disputes as long as they did not adversely affect the progress of the railroad. On May 6, 1869, however, the San Francisco Evening Bulletin *reported a Chinese Tong war requiring the attention of Strobridge:*

A battle has occurred between two rival companies of Chinamen, several hundred in number, laborers of the See Yup and Teng Wo Companies. They have been idle at Victory [a camp], eight miles from here, for a number of days past. The row occurred over $15 due from one camp to the other. After the usual braggadocio, both parties sailed in, at a given signal, armed with every conceivable weapon. Spades were handled and crowbars, spikes, picks and infernal machines were hurled between the rank of the contestants. Several shots were fired and everything betokened the outbreak of a riot. At this juncture, Superintendent Strobridge, with several of his men, rushed into the melee and, with the assistance of the leading "Chinamen," who were more peaceably disposed, he succeeded in separating the combatants and restoring order.

nal societies in China, when they functioned in American cities such as San Francisco, Sacramento, and the railroad camps, criminal activities were significantly reduced in favor of providing support for their members.

Functioning as protective associations, each provided a multitude of services to its members new to California and suffering from homesickness and fears of how they would be treated by the whites who openly expressed racial animosity toward them. As contemporary historian Thomas W. Chinn summed up the workings of the Six Companies, "They provided what white society did not or would not provide."[22]

Once the new arrivals settled in the camps, the Six Companies helped them adjust to the confusing foreign work environment by providing information about the rules of the camp, where to find what they needed, and generally how to stay out of trouble. Later, the companies might provide legal assistance, medical treatment, mail service to relatives in China, and employment opportunities for family members wishing to work in California. On occasion, Tongs secondarily functioned as insurance firms, bankers, marriage brokers, and concubine purveyors.

On October 10, 1865, Leland H. Stanford, one of the principal owners of the Central Pacific, had these complimentary observations to make about the Six Companies in a report to President Andrew Johnson:

Leland Stanford, an owner of the Central Pacific, admired the organizational structure of the Chinese Tongs.

> We find them organized into societies for mutual aid and assistance. These societies can count their numbers by thousands, are conducted by shrewd, intelligent businessmen who promptly advise their subordinates where employment can be found on most favorable terms. Their wages, which are always paid in coin each month, are divided among them by their agents who attend to their business according to the labor done by each person. These agents are generally American or Chinese merchants who furnish them their supplies of food, the value of which they deduct from their monthly pay.[23]

After paying for their food, the average Chinese worker saved an estimated twenty dollars a month, most of which was sent back to San Francisco by their Tong to Chinese-owned banks. Most Chinese had one or two intended uses for their savings: They would send it home so when they returned to China at some future time they would have money to buy a farm, or they would stay in America and purchase a business. Tongs assisted their members in purchasing such businesses and protecting them from attack by anti-Chinese citizens.

WORK CREW ORGANIZATIONS

In addition to the social Tong societies, the Chinese workers further organized themselves into work crews of between twelve and thirty men. Unlike the white work crews that gathered each morning to work on a particular task such as surveying or rail setting, Chinese work crews also provided personal services to their own members.

Each Chinese crew selected one of its members to act as a full-time cook and a second to act as a general attendant to administer to all of the crew's other personal needs. Since these two men did not work directly on the construction of the railroad nor were they paid by the railroad, their wages were paid by the other members of the crew—each receiving about one dollar per month from each crew member.

Each of the estimated five hundred cooks catering to the culinary needs of the twelve thousand Chinese workers shopped, cooked, and provided

A worker carries tea to his Chinese coworkers, one of many services the Chinese Tongs provided to crews.

hot tea all day long for his crew. The exotic foods they prepared were either imported from China or were found along California's coastline or bountiful agricultural valleys. The cooks made out long lists of foods that were ordered by the Central Pacific, shipped up to the campsites, and stocked in the last four railroad cars hitched to the camp train. These were used exclusively as mobile stores for the purchase of food by the Chinese cooks. Invoices that have survived from that time indicate an enormous volume of unusual seafoods and vegetables probably never eaten by the white crews.

The attendants, who were often chosen because of their ability to speak a little English, performed a number of functions. Perhaps of greatest concern was to receive and disperse the men's salaries. Every payday when the men's money was

Chinese workers and a white overseer ride a construction train carrying wood.

distributed by the railroad, each attendant would gather his crew's share of the coins, pay himself, disperse four or five dollars to each man, and send the remainder to the bank. When disputes arose because the men believed they had not been fairly paid, it was the job of the attendants to argue the point with the railroad.

A daily task was to carry food and hot tea to the workmen. Many of the photographs taken by journalists and railroad historians show the attendants carrying two buckets of tea or food balanced on either end of a long pole carried over their shoulders. Next in importance was their job of preparing hot baths for the men at the end of the day before the evening meal.

HEALTH AND HYGIENE

The baths meant more to the Chinese than the immediate comfort of warm water high in the chilly Sierras. Virtually every newspaper writer and Central Pacific manager who commented on the general health of the railroad crews noted that the Chinese seemed far healthier than their white counterparts. Personal hygiene played a major role in maintaining their superior health. Their evening baths combined with their insistence on washing their clothes at least once a week—far more frequently than white workers—kept their skin free of the rashes and sores commonly found on the other men.

Their varied diet of healthy seafoods, vegetables, fruits, and other highly nutritious items was just as important as hygiene for good health. Robert F.G. Spier quotes an early California historian who noted while visiting them that because of their healthy diet, the Chinese lived "Far better, and at any rate have a more varied bill of fare than most of the ranch men of California. Compare this bill of fare with the beef, beans, bread and butter, and potatoes of the white laborers, and you will see that John [the Chinese] has a much healthier variety of food."[24]

Tea was another health factor. Many nineteenth-century historians pointed out that instead of drinking contaminated water drawn from nearby lakes and rivers, the Chinese drank warm tea that initially had been boiled. Whether they did this to purify the water intentionally or not is unknown; however, the effect was that they suffered less from intestinal diseases such as dysentery and cholera than crew members who drank water from local sources.

The healthy regimen of the Chinese could not guarantee perfect health, however. When the first few men became ill, they refused to trust Western doctors and demanded that the railroad hire a Chinese herbalist named Yee Fung Cheung to attend to their medical needs. While working as an herbalist for the railroad,

---

❧ A CHILLING DISCOVERY ❧

Winter work conditions claimed many lives. The exact number is unknown because the Central Pacific did not keep records and because some who died in avalanches were never found. The spring thaw often uncovered those who had died during the winter and on rare occasions, other crews discovered frozen workers still buried in the snow. George Kraus, in his book High Road to Promontory: Building the Central Pacific (now the Southern Pacific) Across the High Sierra, *reports on one such discovery made by a group of managers. What makes this discovery interesting to historians is the manner in which the white railroad managers disposed of the dead Chinese worker:*

There was a dance at Donner Lake at a hotel, and a sleigh load of us went up from Truckee and on our return, about 9 A.M. next morning, we saw something under the tree by the side of the road, it's shape resembling that of a man. We stopped and found a frozen Chinese. As a consequence, we threw him in the sleigh with the rest of us, and took him into town and laid him out by the side of a shed and covered him with a rice mat, the most appropriate thing for the laying out of a Celestial [Chinese].

Yee scoured the forests for herbal remedies for his men and also played a role in determining their diet and hygiene.

DINNER

Quitting time each workday came when one of the crew foremen hollered as loudly as possible down the construction line, "Time." Filthy and tired, the men wandered back into camp, stacked their tools, and looked forward to an evening of rest and relaxation. With only three or four hours before going to sleep, this was their most treasured time of the day.

Mealtime for a member of a Chinese crew on the Central Pacific was unlike anything the Irish crews on the Union Pacific could possibly imagine. Before dinner, each took a bath, either a simple sponge bath or in a powder keg filled with hot water, and then changed into clean blue cotton pants, a flopping-sleeved quilted shirt, sandals, and a large circular straw hat. Next he sat down with his group and waited to be served his meal by the group's servers.

The Chinese demanded, and received at their own expense, delicacies never seen, let alone tasted, by the white crews. The Chinese menu included such exotic dishes as dried and salted fish, abalone, squid, dried seaweed, bamboo shoots, mushrooms, chicken, and pork, along with large assortments of fruits as wells as eggs, tomatoes, and pickles shipped to them from the California's San Joaquin Valley. The dinner was finished with tea steeped in scoured empty powder kegs that earned the tea its name "gunpowder tea."

EVENING ACTIVITIES

Following their dinner, according to historian Robert West Howard, the Chinese would sit around their campfires, "humming songs or chirping like angry orioles around a fan-tan [gambling] game."[25] The Chinese enjoyed gambling as much as the rest of the white crews, and Howard adds that they "wagered wildly and frequently argued fiercely over the results."[26] However animated they might become, bets were kept small and no one was allowed to cheat. Incidents of stealing and fighting were rare, while killing each other over a game was unheard of.

Visitors to the camp observed another evening activity entirely foreign to them. Some of the Chinese would take a small, long-stemmed pipe, pack it with opium, and smoke it. Most of the railroad bosses, politicians, and Christian ministers opposed their use of opium, yet, at the same time, praised

Many Chinese immigrants retained traditional practices such as smoking opium.

them for not indulging in alcohol as was so prevalent among the white workers. Chinese workers used opium primarily for two reasons: for pain relief and to induce a feeling of calm. According to August W. Loomis, a Christian minister who witnessed them smoking the narcotic:

> They do not stupefy themselves with opium, you do not see them intoxicated with it rolling in the gutters like swine, as one saw so many whiskey soaked whites. Instead, the Chinese would smoke a pipe or two on quiet Saturday nights, their eyes glazing over peacefully in their tents, causing no problems for their fellow man. Strobridge and Crocker detested the narcotic but never interrupted its use. It was a tranquil and tranquilizing device, and they let it be.[27]

The crew bosses, who publicly opposed the use of opium, did nothing to stop it because, as one foreman said, "after an eighty-hour week dangling over a cliff edge or hauling rock out of a tunnel mouth, . . . a man deserved his own kind of recreation."[28]

❧ LIVING LIKE MOLES ❧

During the winter of 1866–1867, the volume of snowfall was so great that it was not unusual for a man to step onto freshly fallen snow and to sink up to his shoulders. Such conditions made simple tasks such as walking virtually impossible, let alone performing the work of tunneling and leveling the railbed. To survive and function in such adverse conditions, Chinese workers learned to burrow beneath the snow in order to move about the camp as well as to perform their work. To illuminate these crawl spaces, the Chinese sliced holes through the sides to permit light. Historian George Kraus, in his book High Road to Promontory, *quotes John Gillis, a railroad historian who described the Chinese living and working in these adverse conditions this way:*

The Chinese workers lived like moles, many feet below the surface. They passed from work to living quarters through snow tunnels fifty to two hundred feet long. These tunnels had to be enlarged constantly to prevent them from settling down at the crown. Windows were made at intervals for light and for throwing out excavated materials. The men crowded shoulder to shoulder trying to chip and hack the rock. This was the hardest kind of granite, so hard that as many as five shots of explosives were placed within the small holes chipped in the rock and oftentimes they would have no effect at all.

Sleeping arrangements for the Chinese changed with the seasons. During mild and warm weather, all slept in canvas tents or under the stars with a bedroll consisting of a blanket laid over a bed of pine needles. As the temperature dropped with the changing seasons, a fire kept the men warm until storms rolled in dropping several feet of snow. Following the first snows, the Chinese had no choice but to dig burrows deep into the earth for their sleeping quarters. Sleeping several feet underground, the Chinese lined their burrows with animal skins and thick layers of moss and pine needles that provided comfort and a small amount of insulation from the cold.

In spite of the cultural differences that caused occasional friction between the Chinese and the white workers, the Central Pacific camp operated with a remarkably high degree of harmony. The Chinese were very well received, as Mr. Loomis attested: "They are ready to work the moment they hear the signal, and labor steadily and honestly until admonished that the working hours are ended."[29] This observation was corroborated by Crocker himself who said when testifying before Congress, "The Chinese worked themselves into our favor to such an extent that I would take Chinese labor to do it [difficult work] with, because of their greater reliability and steadiness, and their aptitude and capacity for hard work."[30]

Unfortunately for the Union Pacific railroad, which was working its way west across the Great Plains, the same camp harmony and good-spirited appreciation between management and working crew were less often evidenced.

CAMP LIFE ON THE UNION PACIFIC

Camp life on the Union Pacific had a very different tone from that of the Central Pacific. Although both camps operated in much the same way, providing a mobile site to supply the needs of the men and to disperse construction material, the major challenges for the Union Pacific were very different, as was the ethnic composition of the crew.

The major challenge for the Union Pacific on their drive west across the relatively flat Great Plains between Council Bluffs, Iowa, and Promontory, Utah, was fighting off the Indians who lived directly in the path of the railroad. Although the crews encountered their fair share of logistical problems and camp difficulties, it was the fear of Indian attacks that gave their westward push its character.

An estimated 85 percent of the Union Pacific workers were Irish who had immigrated to America just before the Civil War. Many of the men arrived penniless in New York and readily accepted three hundred dollars to fight in the Civil War in place of Americans who had the money and wished to avoid the conflict. When the war ended, these Irishmen were looking for work and flocked to Iowa to build the railroad.

By all accounts, the Irish were a rough group of men willing to succumb to rowdy drunken behavior that cast a constant pall over camp life. This inclination, coupled with their experiences fighting in the Civil War, made for a camp filled with raucous misconduct. As poet Stephen Vincent Benét wrote:

They were strong men [who] built the Big Road and it was the Irish [that] did it. [They] could swing a pick all day and dance all night, if there was a

❧ GREETING THE INDIANS ❧

On a few rare occasions, there were moments when workers on the Union Pacific were able to peaceably greet the Indians and even show them around their railroad trains. In April 1867 Jack Casement watched seventeen Sioux Indians led by their chief, Spotted Tail, ride right up to the tracks. Casement saw they had come peacefully and decided to take the opportunity to show off the superiority of his men, weapons, and machinery.

Casement invited them into one of the railroad cars stacked with army rifles just to watch the expressions on their faces. But then the expressions changed. As a challenge to the Indians, Casement ordered a shovel to be set in the ground sixty feet from the train and challenged the Indians to try to shoot their arrows through the

hole in the handle. E.C. Lockwood, who witnessed the contest, wrote in *Union Pacific Magazine,* in 1938, "Sixteen of the Indians shot their arrows through the hole in the handle, while the seventeenth hit the handle near the hole, knocking the shovel over. He felt quite disgraced. Casement was sobered by their accuracy."

Next Casement proposed a race between the Indians on their horses and the locomotive. Lockwood recalled the race, saying, "At first the Indians outdistanced the locomotive, which so pleased them that they gave their Indian war whoop. But presently the engine gathered speed, then overhauled them. The engineer as the train past opened his whistle, which so startled them that all, as if by word of command, swung to the off-side of their ponies."

fiddler handy. They liked the strength and wildness of it—would drink with the thirstiest and fight with the wildest. It was all meat and drink to them.[31]

TOUGH AND ROWDY CAMP CONDITIONS

Union Pacific hands had no alternative but to live tough. Lacking any semblance of privacy or civility in the camps that moved down the line a mile or two each day, every man

faced a daily struggle to stay alive and to keep up with the grueling work schedule. Unlike the Chinese, Irish workers did not organize; every man fended for himself.

Workers had to be prepared to fight for everything they had. Without the protection of laws and law enforcement officers, only the tough survived. Payday presented each man with the agony of protecting his gold coins that could not be safely stashed anywhere other than in his

A Union Pacific workers' camp. Such places were often the scene of robberies and dangerous, drunken brawls.

pants pockets. Banking arrangements did not exist as they did for the Chinese. This unsettling situation forced most to sleep with their pants on or to hide their money in a small bag that they placed under their heads while they slept. Regardless of how carefully the men protected their gold, robbery was a constant reality. One of the few workers to write a diary, Arthur Ferguson, recorded one evening, "Quite a number of bullets whistled over my head. This evening, or afternoon, rather, a man was shot through the head and robbed of quite a sum of money."[32]

Many of the bloodiest fights and killings along the rail lines did not involve Indians. Much, if not most, of the rowdy behavior exhibited by railroad workers involved alcohol. The alcohol problem became so acute on the Union Pacific that one of the superintendents ordered an end to drinking on the job because of the number of accidents. He ordered all men to surrender their bottles and whiskey flasks, which were whimsically referred to as "pocket pistols."

Alcohol or not, murders in camps were regular occurrences. An official photographer for the Union Pacific arrived to photograph and comment on anything he believed might be of historical interest. As part of the photographer's story that he filed, he noted the nature of camp deaths:

> In sight of their camp was the beautiful city of Deadfall and Last Chance. I was creditably informed that 24 men had been killed in the several camps in the last 25 days. Certainly a harder set of men were never congregate together before . . . Every ranch or tent has whiskey for sale. Verily, men earn their money like horses and spend it like asses.[33]

But there was a limit to rowdy behavior. Union Pacific bosses ruled with an iron fist. Any time problematic behavior impacted the schedule, the railroad sent men to solve the problem and discipline the unruly men. One of the men hired by the railroad and charged with the responsibility for dealing with incorrigible offenders, commented in his diary, "Rode to Brigham City—found camp there. G.L. drunk—had him arrested. Discharged L. Pratt and Van Wagner—drunk. Settled up with George and Walter—the latter I discharged for imprudence."[34]

Self-defense was one part of the equation for survival and another was being able to travel light. The less a man carried, the less he would lose, and the less he had to worry about.

TRAVELING LIGHT

Few workers traveled with little more than the shirts on their backs. As the crews moved forward at a slow but certain pace, any personal items the men brought to camp had to move with them and had to be cared for. Personal items were kept to a bare minimum. A single change of clothing was standard for most men. This pathetic clothing situation is documented by many photographs taken at the time the transcontinental railroad was completed, showing many men still wearing their Civil War uniforms—five years following the conclusion of the war.

Unlike the Chinese on the Central Pacific who bathed and changed clothes regularly, the Union Pacific workers did not. Filth was part of the price paid for traveling light, and the men had grown accustomed to it fighting the Civil War. The only exception to working for months at a stretch without washing clothes were the men who were paid better than the common workers. One bridge engineer, for example, casually mentioned in an engineering report, "I sent my laundry to Omaha, more than five hundred miles away."[35]

Whatever personal items men brought with them had to be compact and sturdy. Many had pocketknives, small metal musical instruments, a deck of cards, and perhaps a pocket watch carrying an inscription. Most favored personal items such as chewing tobacco, candy, and soft drinks could be purchased in camp. Also widely purchased was an assortment of toiletries such as combs, toothbrushes, razors, soap, and pain relievers.

QUITTING TIME

At the end of the workday, all crew members stacked their tools and headed into camp to rest and relax for the rest of the evening. Following a quick wash, the Union Pacific crew lined up to eat dinner, the only meal that the men could eat leisurely. The Great Plains did not yield the bountiful array of foods that California did, but the predominantly Irish crews were typically satisfied to stand in one of several serving lines to receive their portion of beef either carved off a cow roasted on a spit or boiled in a metal water trough. Next along the serving line were fifty-gallon barrels filled with hot beans or potatoes, then wicker baskets filled with bread, and finally hot coffee. As a supplement to this filling but bland diet, women

---

❧ BEAR FOR DINNER ❧

Locating adequate food to feed the crews was a constant problem faced by both railroads. In addition to seeming never to have enough for the enormous appetites of the crews, there was the issue of trying to find different foods to keep the men happy. One day late in the afternoon when Major General Grenville M. Dodge return to camp, he asked the cook about the whereabouts of a couple of men he wanted to talk to. The cook said that they had gone out to follow a grizzly bear that had passed through the camp a short time ago and hoped that they would be able to shoot it and bring it back to camp for dinner. Irritated by what he considered a dangerous and reckless undertaking, Dodge retold the story in his book

How We Built the Union Pacific Railway:

It was but a short time until we heard two shots and in few minutes afterwards we saw Rawlins and Dunn coming towards us with the greatest speed. I knew then they had shot at the bear and had wounded him and he was following them. As Rawlins and Dunn came up I saw the bear was close and I drew the bear's attention giving me a very good shot, but I hit him a little too far back, but did not stop him. Sol Gee waited until he got him face-to-face and then shot him between the eyes and dropped him. He was one of the largest grizzlies I ever saw.

At the end of a long day, Union Pacific laborers share a leisurely dinner and relax.

from small towns along the way occasionally sold fresh baked goods to the crews. Recognizing that homemade goods boosted morale, railroad officials purchased fresh bread, doughnuts, pies, and milk.

When the boredom of railroad food set in on the Union Pacific, workers sometimes had the option of eating dinner at one of several restaurant tents. These restaurants were privately owned by people willing to travel behind the railroad crews, set up tents, and cook every

evening to feed the men. Bearing names such as "City Bakery," "Montana House," and "Mom's Cooking," each provided filling home-cooked meals that cost each man fifty cents—the equivalent of two or three hours of work.

Following dinner and coffee, the men gathered in their social groups for an hour or so of rest and simple forms of entertainment. Sitting by evening fires and kerosene lamps, the men of the Union Pacific had only a few choices for entertainment before

In mild weather, workers usually slept in white canvas tents.

turning in for sleep. Men tended to gather and play a variety of card games; some gambling games cost men their hard-earned money, but others were strictly for amusement. Songs were more popular than cards, and men would pull out small, simple instruments such as Jew's harps and harmonicas that could be easily packed away. The songs that were most popular were simple regional folk favorites and tunes from the Civil War.

When the campfires were extinguished, the men scattered to find a place to sleep. When the weather was favorable, crews typically pitched white canvas tents that would be broken down after daybreak, packed on wagons, and hauled down the road where they would be reassembled for the next night's sleep. The size of each tent was roughly twenty by twenty feet, which was large enough to accommodate ten to fifteen men. During winters, the railroads supplied prefabricated wood buildings that provided drier accommodations. Each piece of these buildings was numbered for rapid assembly and disassembly.

Winter weather created problems for sleep. Many of the crew chose to sleep in large dormitory cars that were attached to the camp train. Photos of these cars show them to be much larger than any of the other cars. Eighty-five feet long, ten feet high, and ten feet wide, they were so long that they sagged in the middle, earning them the nickname of "swaybacks." These dormitory cars were capable of accommodating 180 bunks. Short on privacy, the bunks were nonetheless fought over during the winters because there were not enough to accommodate everyone. Since they filled up quickly, many of the latecomers were forced to sleep outside during mild weather. The men became adept at making basic mattresses out of natural products such as pine needles, buffalo skins, and ropes stretched in a crosshatch pattern suspended a few inches above the ground. When the temperature dropped, fires were built and tended throughout the night.

CAMP FOLLOWERS

Following the railroad camps down the line were unscrupulous entrepreneurs who looked upon this twelve-thousand-man construction crew of lonely young men as a golden opportunity to get rich. Unloading tents from their wagons each night, they set up a small tent city of saloons, gambling dens, and bordellos. Known to everyone on the Union Pacific as "Hell on Wheels," this circus followed the railroad from start to finish.

Most workdays the crewmen stayed in camp for the evening but on Saturday night and Sunday, the one day off of the week, crews found their way to a variety of forms of entertainment provided by camp followers. American historians state emphatically that few Union Pacific railroad workers ever returned home at the completion of the transcontinental railroad with so much as a dime in their pockets.

Hell on Wheels perfected the strategy of getting the men drunk and then taking their money by one ruse or another. These traveling tent businesses exemplified the Wild West and were operated by the sleazier elements of society. Whiskey, the preferred alcoholic drink of the crews, sold in the tent saloons for between fifty and seventy-five cents a shot, one-quarter of a man's daily pay and ten times the price paid in Omaha. And even at those inflated prices, the whiskey was half water. Nonetheless, plenty of patrons were willing to down the Red Dog, Red Cloud, Blue Run, and Red Eye whiskies.

According to an observer who witnessed many of these tent saloons, "It could almost be said that the Union Pacific was built on whiskey and whiskey watered the weed-choked gardens of prostitution, gambling, and general mayhem and depravity"[36] Its debilitating effect on the Union Pacific working crews caused more deaths directly or indirectly than Indian attacks or construction accidents.

GAMBLING

Once the men were intoxicated, the gambling tents took their turn emptying the men's pockets of whatever remained of their monthly pay. One reporter traveling to experience one of these tent cities described the owners as "a carnivorous horde hungrier than the native prairie grasshoppers, ready, able, and willing to nibble on wads of Union Pacific greenbacks."[37] The saloon owners, not surprisingly, usually operated the gambling tents that brought in more money than did whiskey. Once the railroaders were tipsy, the card dealers were able to cheat them without being caught.

British journalist Henry Morton Stanley wrote about the gambling epidemic that never failed to clean out the young workers: "Every house is a saloon and every saloon is a gambling den. Revolvers are in great requisition. Beardless youths try their hands at the 'Mexican Monte,' 'high-low-Jack,' 'strap,' 'rouge-et-noir,' 'chuck-a-luck,' and lose their all."[38]

When the drunken rail setters realized too late that their month's wages were gone, many made the additional mistake of accusing the dealers of cheating. With that, pis-

A construction train is pictured in a small town along the route. On weekends, Union Pacific workers frequented brothels and bars like the one at right.

Intoxicated rail workers often lost their wages in gambling establishments.

tols were drawn and fired. Death in back alleys was a common Saturday night occurrence.

Head engineer Maj. Gen. Grenville M. Dodge, who hated these unseemly places and personally refused to patronize them, wrote the following note to his wife about what he saw:

> The next place visited was a gambling hall where all games of chance were being played. Men excited with drink and dally were recklessly staking their last dollar on the turn of the card or the throw of a dice.

Women were cajoling and coaxing tipsy men to stake their money on various games; the pockets were shrewdly picked by the fallen women or the more sober of the crowd.[39]

PROSTITUTION

After visiting the saloons and casinos, any money left over was spent on the women who set up their tents along with all the others. Journalist Henry Morton Stanley described one such tent, which was also used as a dance hall:

☙ HELL ON WHEELS ❧

Like it or not, the railroad companies had to recognize that each Hell on Wheels catered to their workmen in ways the railroad companies could not. And like it or not, the railroad companies had to recognize that the people working at these establishments of vice were very much part of the construction environment even though they were not employed by the railroads. Historian John Hoyt Williams, in his book A Great and Shining Road, *documents many observations made by writers who saw the entertainers working in the little city of Benton, Wyoming:*

This was Benton, averaging a murder a day; gambling and drinking, hurdy-gurdy dancing, and the violence of sexual commerce. . . . These bad men and lewd women continued to leapfrog the Union Pacific's work crews, catching the drippings from the feast in any and every form that it was possible to reach them . . . desperadoes of every grade, the vilest of men and women . . . this congregation of scum and wickedness trekked ever westward, harbinger of civilization as much as were the surveyors, graders, and track men who sampled their delights.

The hall was crowded with bad men and lewd women. Such profanity, vulgarity and indecency as was heard and seen there would disgust a more hardened person than I. These women are expensive articles, and come in for a large share of the money wasted. In broad daylight they may be seen gliding through sandy streets in Black Crook dresses, carrying fancy derringers slung to their waists, with such tools they are dangerously expert.[40]

Major General Dodge recalled a problem that had arisen in the city of Julesburg where each night several of his workmen had been found shot to death following disputes over money and women. Outraged by the loss of manpower, Dodge ordered Casement to confront the owners of the bordellos and saloons with armed men and to demand that deaths come to an end. The confrontation ended in a gun battle killing many of the owners. Dodge later asked Casement about the outcome of the incident and reported: "When I returned to Julesburg, I asked General Casement what he had done. He replied, 'I will show you.' He took me up to a little rise just beyond Julesburg and showed me a small graveyard saying, 'General they all died in their boots, but brought peace.'"[41]

Camp life was largely determined by the men and how they chose to live, relax, spend their money, and associate with their friends. Life on the construction lines, however, was another matter. When the men reported for work each morning, six days a week, they were expected to take orders and contribute to the construction of the railroad.

CHAPTER 4

SPECIALTY CREWS AND SPECIAL DANGERS ON THE UNION PACIFIC

Crew members on the Union Pacific often commented that, with the exception of the war, no other job presented greater dangers nor generated greater fear than building the rail- road. Many succumbed to illness and disease, some died as a result of dangers inherent in the construction of tunnels and bridges, while others died from the arrows and scalping

An Indian gazes down a valley in which the newly laid rail line parallels a river. Determined to prevent construc- tion of the rail- road, Indians often killed rail workers, who likened the dangers of their job to those of war.

↝ SCALPED ALIVE ↜

Railroad workers had many reasons to live in constant fear. Many Native American tribes scalped railroad workers they captured in hand-to-hand combat. As the Union Pacific railroad crews worked, the telegraph company followed, setting their telegraph lines. The Indians knew that if they cut the wires, a repair crew would arrive within a day to make repairs. One day a band of Cheyenne cut the lines and awaited the repair crew. When they arrived on a small train, all were immediately killed except William Thompson who survived the attack. The British journalist Henry Morton Stanley relates in his book, The Autobiography of Sir Henry Morton Stanley, *that he later encountered Thompson who told him that one Cheyenne Indian rode him down "and clubbed me with his rifle. He then took out his knife, stabbed me in the neck, and making a twirl around his fingers with my hair, he commenced sawing and* hacking away at my scalp." Feigning death, Thompson knew "enough to keep quiet."

"After what seemed like an hour, my scalp was simply ripped off by the impatient Cheyenne—it just felt as if the whole head was taken off." Lying there dazed and bleeding, he noticed that his "scalp fell with a plop to the ground" as the Indian remounted his horse. When the Indian rode off, Thompson put his scalp in a pail of water. Stanley continued, "in a pail of water by his side, was his scalp, about nine inches in length and four in width, somewhat resembling a drowned rat." Later Stanley continued the gruesome story saying that Thompson took his scalp to doctors to "reset the scalp on his head, almost as if it were prairie sod but the painful operation failed, to his disappointment."

knives of the Indians who refused to allow the "Iron Horse," as they referred to the locomotives, to trespass across their lands without a fight.

RAILROADERS AND INDIAN FIGHTERS

The men of the Union Pacific may have signed on to lay rails, but railroad managers had more than that in mind. Management knew that Indians would aggressively defend their territory. They further knew that crews were sure to die. While working their way through Indian Territory, railroad crews also became Indian fighters.

Several months before the first rails were laid by the Union Pacific, the British journalist Henry Morton Stanley was traveling throughout Nebraska with the Union Pacific surveying crews and sent a column to his newspaper with the jarring observation

Indians attack a construction crew. Rail workers lived in constant fear of such attacks, which frequently involved torture and scalping.

that within a thirty-one-mile stretch of land surveyed by the Union Pacific, he had encountered "No less than ninety-three graves; twenty-seven of which contained the bodies of settlers killed within the last six weeks. Dead bodies have been seen floating down the Platte [River]."[42]

The relentless Indian attacks were costly in terms of men's lives and the railroad's money. Attacks on the crews were generally small and sporadic, yet unpredictable and constant. At no time were the crews far from their own rifles or from the protection of the United States military. Maj. Gen. Grenville M. Dodge suc-

cinctly explained the gravity of the problem this way:

Our Indian troubles commenced in 1864 and lasted until the tracks jointed Promontory. We lost most of our men and stock while building from Fort Kearney [Nebraska] to Bitter Creek [Wyoming]. At that time every mile of road had to be surveyed, graded, tied, and bridged under military protection. The order to every surveying corps, grading, building and tie outfit was never to run when attacked. All were required to be armed, and I do not know that the order was disobeyed in a single instance.[43]

Surveyors, who worked many miles in advance of the large rail-setting crews, were terrified of Indian attacks because of the Indian custom of scalping and mutilating their victims while still alive. A doctor who treated five men shot with arrows commented in his report, "One of the men killed was lying on the ground, pinned to the earth by an arrow through his neck; he must have been shot after he had been scalped."[44] One railroad man who was killed received a tombstone with an epitaph written by a semiliterate companion that read, "Here lyes, Jeemes Engles, hoo was kild by the

---

ꙮ AN INDIAN ATTACK ꙮ

The principal reason that work crews deserted the Union Pacific was fear of the Indians—not just fear of losing their lives, but also fear of being scalped alive. These fears were especially prevalent among surveying and grading crews that worked several miles ahead of the main camp. As gruesome stories of scalpings circulated among the crews, fewer and fewer men were willing to volunteer to join small work details.

In June 1867 young surveyor named Arthur Ferguson recorded a chilling Indian attack in his surveying notes. Its historical significance rests with it being one of the few actual records of Indian attacks and of interest on the part of the whites in scalping Indians. The incident is found in David Howard Bain's book, Empire Express, *and begins with the shouts:*

"'Here they come, there they come boys!' And everyone in the tents scram- bled out of their sleeping bags, grabbing rifles and bits of clothing emerging to see a mounted raiding party cantering down upon them from the northern bluffs. Some of our men were almost naked, I had nothing on but shirt, drawers and stockings. Rifle fire erupted all through the camp, wreathing it in blue smoke."

Moments later, Ferguson commented on an Indian who had stolen their horses and while attempting to escape, "A bullet strikes him, he sways to and fro in his saddle, as if the force of the bullet came very near to dismounting him; another shot strikes him, he reels and falls to the ground." But, just at this moment when one of the railroad workers moved in to finish him off, other Indians swooped in to save his life and as the raiding party rode off, Ferguson lamented, "We lost the chance of getting a fine scalp."

Shy-An injuns. Juli 1800 and 68. He was a good egg."[45] Following several such killings, Dodge issued an order calling on his men to aggressively respond to such incidents:

> Place every mounted man in your command on the South Platte route [Nebraska]; repair telegraph lines, attack all bodies of hostile Indians large or small; stay with them and pound them until they move north of the Platte [River] or south of the Arkansas [River]. I am coming with two regiments of the cavalry to the Platte line and will open and protect it.[46]

Between 1867 and 1868, many tribes made quick attacks against the railroad crews. Usually the story was the same: The Native Americans would capture and torture the workmen and then run off. An occasional twist to such quick attacks was the theft of cattle that the railroad kept to feed the men. Cattle herds were tended by one of the more unusual crews associated with both railroads: cowboys.

COWBOYS AND THE RAILROAD

One of the more unusual specialty crews on the Union Pacific moving down the rails side by side with the locomotives were cowboys. Once the Union Pacific reached its full labor complement, beef became the primary staple that fueled the twelve-thousand-man crew. Beef was served in one form or another at all three meals, which meant that tons of the high protein food was consumed daily. The best way to provide gargantuan quantities of beef while moving was to hire cowboys to herd cattle down the line along with all the other provisions and equipment needed to build the railroad.

The first large herd was purchased in Omaha, and as it was depleted, more head were purchased from the few homesteaders in Nebraska who dared settle in Indian country. Later, as the railroad moved deeper into Indian Territory, the herds were replenished by shipping cattle forward to join the herd. Feeding on the lush, tall grasses of the prairie, the cattle remained fat until butchered and roasted for one of the day's meals.

Winter on the range created problems for the cowboys. As snowdrifts deepened, locating sufficient grazing grounds for the cattle became difficult and the cattle lost weight. Unlike the indigenous buffalo that were capable of pawing through ice and snow to find enough to eat, the cattle wandered aimlessly and eventually starved. The railroad solved this problem by sending trains forward with flatcars stacked high with bales of hay. Although this appeared to be a reasonable solution to the problem, it had its problems.

During the winter of 1867, a train hauling bales of hay caught fire from embers from the wood-burning locomotive. At first a bale or two, then the entire carload, and finally several carloads were blazing. On board one of the passenger cars was Arthur Ferguson, a surveyor for the railroad, who recalled the fiery incident this way: "It was a grand sight to see an engine rushing madly across the plains, followed by a car wrapped in flames and streaming sparks and fire in its path. We had to run with these burning cars some ten to twelve miles."[47]

SNOW HAZARDS AND SNOW REMOVAL CREWS

Winters on the prairie often slowed the work crews and occasionally brought them to a halt. When snowdrifts were high, supply trains were stopped in their tracks, stranding badly needed supplies. Trains that were stranded for days jeopardized

Harsh winter weather impeded construction and delayed the arrival of supplies.

the lives of all on board and delayed the completion of the railroad.

Initially, when the drifts were small, all passengers riding stranded trains were compelled to grab shovels and clear the snow, foot by foot, until they had worked their way through the drift. In response to complaints about this, the Union Pacific placed teams of strong young men on the snow removal crews who rode the trains specifically to shovel for an entire day or more, if necessary, to free a train.

When the snows worsened, the shoveling crews took on a second task of fitting a wedge-shaped ram, called a "bucker plow," on the front of their engines. These plows functioned as battering rams to force their way through snowdrifts taller than the locomotives. When the heavy, compacted snow eventually stopped the locomotive, the engineer backed up the train a mile or two and then rammed it, hoping to push through. More often than not, however, the shoveling crews had to begin the tedious manual task of removing the snow.

Better technology was needed. The railroad heard about a new invention called a "rotary snowplow" that was a boxcar fitted on one end with a set of large circular blades rotating on a shaft, much like a fan, parallel to the tracks. As the engine pushed the rotary plow down the track, the ten-foot-diameter spinning blades tossed snow aside with astonishing speed. During the last winter of 1868, the snow removal crews mounted the experimental rotating plows on all trains. Although this new technology revolutionized railroad travel in snow, the shoveling crews continued to ride the trains to remove the snow manually when the mechanical whirling blades broke.

LUMBER-SCAVENGING CREWS

The Union Pacific was in constant need of supplies and materials to keep construction moving. Failure to maintain stockpiles of critical materials meant suspending work and idling the crew on the entire operation. The most critical material shortage that plagued the Union Pacific from start to finish was a severe lack of lumber for ties and bridges. Thick stands of hardwood trees did not grow across the water-starved prairies. To prevent a costly shutdown, the railroad maintained a small but clever team of lumber scavenger crews whose job was to locate and acquire desperately needed hardwoods any way they could.

Thomas C. Durant, a director of the Union Pacific, was aware of the problem and sent out scavenging crews to scour the northern states in search of good quality lumber wherever they might find it. Frustrated by the delay and their inability to locate the needed timber, one of his scavenging crews found and ordered three hundred thousand hardwood ties, enough to carry the rails the first 120 miles, delivered to Omaha without first asking the price. Durant's initial reaction of elation with his crew's resourcefulness changed to fury when he later received the exorbitant bill for $1.3 million.

Once beyond the 120-mile mark, the railroad was again plagued by a shortage of ties. In January 1867 Durant sent his scavenging teams in search of lumber in northern Nebraska where they located a dense stand of hardwood trees belonging to the state. Without seeking the permission of the governor, the team cut down enough to mill them into forty thousand ties. In July the ties were floated downstream where they were fished out of the water and used to continue the railroad into Wyoming.

The blatant theft of lumber was eventually uncovered but not forgotten or forgiven. Historian J. Sterling Morton expressed considerable anger toward the Union Pacific in 1881 when he published his *History of Nebraska* noting: "The destruction of our finest forests—and especially of our precious hardwood trees—will always be resented as an act of vandalism which no exigency such as they might plead could excuse or palliate."[48]

Eventually the Union Pacific was forced to turn to the inferior soft cottonwoods. The answer to the problem, at least for the short term, was found by a scavenger crew that discovered a machine called a Burnettizer, named after the inventor. This device was a huge fifty-five-ton cylinder, one hundred feet long and five feet in diameter. Ties were loaded into the machine and a vacuum created to suck the water out of the cells of the wood. Following the extraction of the water, chemicals were injected to give the ties added strength before they were dried. The Burnettizer saved the Union Pacific from bankruptcy by reducing the cost of each tie to a mere sixteen cents, substantially below the price Durant had paid for the hardwood ties.

CAMP TRAIN CREWS

The Union Pacific railroad camps revolved closely around the camp train that served as the nerve center for the entire operation. The camp trains consisted of as many as thirty specially constructed railroad cars, each up to eighty feet long, which functioned as shops providing support for the crews as they moved down the rails. In 1868 a newspaper reporter inspecting the camp train provided this bit of insight into how the entire camp train moved along with construction:

Camp equipment, work shops, boarding houses, offices and in fact the big settlement literally took up its bed and walked. The place that knew it in the morning knew it no more at night. It was miles off and what was a busy town of 5,000 inhabitants in the morning, was a deserted village site at night, while a smooth, well-built, compact road bed for traveling stretched from the morning site to evening tarrying place.[49]

When the Casement army of ten thousand crew members headed west, an estimated one thousand of them worked in a dozen crews that supported the work of the other nine thousand.

The majority of the train crews repaired broken tools or made new ones. The most important and largest crews for making metal repairs were the blacksmiths, tin shapers, boilermakers, and machinists. Of these crews, the blacksmith crew was the largest and busiest. Two cars were dedicated to eight large, hot forges operating all day long. The tools in most constant need of repair or sharpening were the chisels and drill

Camp trains moved along the rails laid each day to reach that night's resting place. This routine was repeated day after day.

Since construction trains could travel only after new rail had been laid, horses and mules were used to move men and materials ahead of the trains.

bits used to drill through granite. Picks, sledgehammers, and shovels were also in constant need of repair or modification for special needs. In addition to the iron tools, ten blacksmiths focused exclusively on shoeing all of the horses and mules used to pull wagons.

The carpenters' car, like that of the blacksmiths' car, was a place for repairs and construction of unusual tools. Wood had to be acquired along the trail, which made it a scarce and valuable material. Building wood trestles across rivers, repairing broken wood wagon wheel spokes, and replacing the wood handles on the picks and shovels kept these men busy.

Horses and mules were indispensable for moving men and material forward, ahead of the trains. More than a thousand of these animals had many special needs that were attended to by teamster crews that not only drove the animals during the day but cared for them in the evening. The most common source of horse ailments was their hooves. Treatment commonly involved clipping, cleaning, and freeing hooves of rot that was common in wet terrain. Sick animals visited the veterinarian's car that had stalls for sick and injured animals as well as a supply room well stocked with remedies and limited operating instruments.

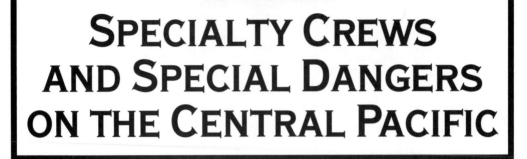

CHAPTER 5

SPECIALTY CREWS AND SPECIAL DANGERS ON THE CENTRAL PACIFIC

To triumph over the Sierras was the single most commanding obstacle on the Central Pacific's segment of the transcontinental railroad. Solving all of the problems that the engineers encountered in the Alpine topography meant, among other things, finding and training specialty crews capable of performing highly unusual tasks not commonly associated with standard railroad construction. Fortunately for the Central Pacific, the Chinese always seemed willing to step forward. Their enthusiasm for all sorts of unusual and often dangerous work was noted in 1865 by a railroad reporter who wrote about the Chinese:

> They are laying siege to Nature in her strongest citadel . . . the rugged mountains look like anthills. They swarm with Celestials [Chinese], shoveling, wheeling,

carting, drilling, and blasting rocks and earth, while their dull mooney eyes stare out from under immense basket hats in shape and size like umbrellas.[50]

The most interesting and sometimes colorful specialty crews unique to the Central Pacific were those associated with tunneling, dangerous railbed construction, bridge building, and logging.

TUNNELING CREWS

Tunneling was the most complicated, risky, dreaded, and dangerous work on either railroad. Of the two railroads, the Central Pacific was forced to do far more of it because of the extent and inconsistency of the terrain over the Sierra mountains. Efficient crews that were capable of laying several miles of track a day across the flat prairies with little work-related peril were slowed to several inches a day when dynamiting through granite mountains.

Digging bores, the term engineers use for the actual holes through the mountain, was well organized but complex and hazardous. Tunnels were so complicated that boring them was one of the few tasks requiring two unrelated crews to work side by side to assure success: tunnel engineers and tunnel blasters. This unusual combination of skills was necessary because boring through mountains was accomplished, in all cases but one, with two blasting crews starting at opposite sides of the mountain boring toward the center. This dicey approach was necessary to speed up the job, yet it created the

❧ VALUES TO BE ADMIRED ❧

Chinese railroad workers did not allow the resentment, ridicule, and persecution expressed by the predominantly Irish white crew members to deter them from learning to survive and even to excel at their jobs. Once the Chinese were given a chance to prove themselves to the Central Pacific, the bosses quickly increased the number of Chinese on the job and gave them additional responsibilities, even though the Irish workers never accepted the responsibilities of the Chinese.

As more and more journalists and other interested citizens visited the railroad camps and observed the behavior of the Chinese, most concurred that their values were more admirable than those of the white crews on either railroad company. August W. Loomis, one of the few Christian ministers to hike up the Sierras to the railroad camp, wrote about the Chinese in an article quoted in Stephen E.

Ambrose's book, *Nothing Like It in the World: The Men Who Built the Transcontinental Railroad 1863–1869:* "They are ready to begin work at the moment they hear the signal, and labor steadily and honestly until admonished that the working hours are ended. Not having acquired a taste for whiskey, they have few fights and no 'blue Mondays.'"

Loomis's view was shared by most managers. George Kraus, in his book *High Road to Promontory,* cites Crocker's appreciation for the work ethic and dedication of the Chinese, which was shared by most upper-level managers: "A large part of our force are Chinese, and they prove equal to white men, in the amount of labor they perform, and are far more reliable. No danger of strikes among them. We are training them to all kinds of labor, blasting, driving horses, handling rock, as well as the pick and shovel."

Tunneling through a mountain was a complicated process. Success depended on holes bored by crews on opposite sides of the mountain meeting in the center.

possibility that the two bores might not meet in the center.

The sole exception to the standard double bore was tunnel No. 6, also known as Summit Tunnel. Tunnel No. 6 was the longest on the entire transcontinental railroad, 1,659 feet, and for this reason four bores took place simultaneously. Two teams bored from each end toward the center as was the case for all tunnels, but the new twist on No. 6 was the addition of more teams boring from the center toward each end. To accomplish this feat, the precise center of the mountain above the proposed tunnel was located and a shaft, large enough to accommodate two teams digging in opposite directions toward each end, was dug straight down.

The requirement that all four teams must meet could not have been accomplished without the calculations of the tunnel engineers.

TUNNEL ENGINEERS

Calculating each bore of a tunnel was done with a pencil and basic measuring tools. Of all the engineers on the Central Pacific, none was more respected than the lead engineer, Lewis Clement. Bore calculations in the 1860s were a mix of mathematics, geometry, and a good dose of eyeballing that took into account curves and elevation changes.

Once all calculations were finalized, Clement plotted each bore on paper showing the precise direction, elevation, curvature, and meeting point. Failure to properly plot all the bores of a tunnel meant the meeting point might be misaligned, delaying the tunneling effort for months.

Clement knew that blasting was not precise. In order to continuously

Lewis Clement's bore calculations involved both mathematics and his keen powers of observation.

make minor adjustments in the direction, elevation, and curvature of each of the bores, he set up a desk inside each bore of tunnel No. 6. Illuminated by torches and working as far away from the blasting as possible, he worked his calculations and plotted the progress of the four bores on maps that he had drawn to scale. Nonetheless, he frequently heard the blasts and felt the concussions that knocked over his desk on more than one occasion.

The tediously slow work of the tunnel-blasting crews following the plot lines of engineers demanded three shifts working around the clock. The blasting crews were divided into three distinct groups: drillers, blasters, and debris haulers.

TUNNEL-BLASTING CREWS

The inherent dangers associated with blasting through mountains made this work the most avoided by the crews. This reality was underscored by the fact that few if any white workers were willing to risk their lives in the tunnels. One of the engineers for the Central Pacific, John Gillis, described the composition of the tunneling crews this way:

> With the exception of a few white men at the west end of tunnel No. 6, the laboring force was entirely composed of Chinese, with white foremen—the laborers working usually in

three shifts of eight hours each, and the foremen into shifts of 12 hours each. A single foreman, with a gang of thirty to forty men, generally constituted the force at work at each end of the tunnel; of these, twelve to fifteen worked on the heading, and the rest on the bottom, removing material.[51]

To split granite, the drillers first drilled holes using hand drills and sledgehammers. When several rows of holes that would cause a major fracture in the rock had been completed, the blasters brought up barrels of black powder and packed each hole, leaving only a small space for the fuse. At a signal from the foreman, everyone exited the tunnel

---

❧ DRILLING GANGS ❧

Drilling holes in granite was the worst work on the railroad line. Each drilling team consisted of three men. One held the 4-foot-long, 1¾ inch-diameter steel drill in place while the two other men alternated pounding on the end of the drill with sledgehammers weighing between twelve and eighteen pounds. When the hole reached a depth of three or four inches, the men vacated the tunnel while a blaster filled the holes with black powder and a fuse.

A standard tunnel, nineteen feet tall and seventeen feet wide, allowed four drilling crews to work side by side. The process began with the man who held the drill. His job was to hold the sharpened point of the drill firmly in one place while constantly rotating it as fast as possible. As he rotated the drill, one of the other men would swing a sledgehammer, striking the drill on the far end. As the hammer swung to his feet, he would use the momentum of the swing to bring it up behind him again and slam it on the end of the drill a second time. After one minute of applying ten strikes, the second sledgehammer man stepped in to take his ten swings while the other rested.

Only a supper break and occasional five-minute tea breaks relieved this sort of physically draining and psychologically monotonous work. When the holes of all four gangs reached three to four inches, the holes were filled with black powder and the fuses set. All drilling gangs exited the tunnel only to return a few minutes later to resume this hellish work after the dust and rubble settled. As historian Stephen E. Ambrose reminds his readers in *Nothing Like it in the World,* "This was done by all three shifts working around the clock. How many fingers or hands were lost to the hammer we don't know."

A blasting crew sets off an explosion. Premature ignition of a faulty fuse sometimes led to the death or injury of crew members.

except for the men who would ignite the fuses. When the second signal was given to light the fuses, the foreman hollered the warning, "fire in the hole," and drillers poured out of the mouth of the tunnel.

When all went well, which was most of the time, a precious few inches of granite cracked, throwing chunks of granite out of the throat of the tunnel. Before the dust and acrid smoke settled, the debris removal crews entered to haul away the rock and to clear the way for the drillers to start the next assault. Sometimes, however, the fuses were faulty, causing a premature ignition that killed or injured anyone nearby. On March 25, 1869, the *Salt Lake City Desert Evening News* reported:

Blasters are jarring the earth every few minutes with their powder, lifting whole ledges of rock from their long resting places, hurling them hundreds of feet in the air and scattering them around for a half mile in every direction.

A few days ago, four men were preparing a blast by filling a large crevice in a ledge with powder. After pouring in the powder they undertook to work it down with iron bars, the bars striking the rocks caused an explosion; one of the men was blown two or three hundred feet in the air, breaking every bone in his body.[52]

Both railroad companies quickly grew impatient with the slow tunnel-ing process and began experimenting with nitroglycerin, a new, colorless liquid compound known to produce a blast between five and eight times more powerful than that of black powder. Although more rock could be loosened with this new liquid explosive, it carried the disadvantage of being highly volatile.

The slightest jolt or impact to the bottles containing nitroglycerin caused it to spontaneously detonate. Before this new explosive ever found

ﾟ NITROGLYCERIN ﾟ

Although nitroglycerin was first used in 1846, the inventor's name is lost to history. The liquid explosive is a molecule compound containing glycerin, carbon, and a mixture of concentrated sulfuric and nitric acids.

The exceptionally violent power of nitroglycerin, when compared to the black powder used by blaster crews, is in the speed of the reaction. Unlike burning with a flame that needs time to travel through the black powder, nitroglycerin reacts almost instantaneously by a supersonic shock wave passing through the liquid. This instantaneous destruction of all the molecules is called a "detonation," and the resulting rapid expansion of hot gases causes the destructive blast. The power of the hot gases is so intense that one unit of nitroglycerin produces nine units of hot explosive gases that were so successful at cracking granite in railroad tunnels.

The major advantage that nitroglycerin has over black powder, one that blasting crews appreciated, was that no soot or smoke was produced when it detonated. Its biggest disadvantage, however, was its volatility that accidentally killed many.

To make the handling of nitroglycerine safer, a Swedish inventor named Alfred Nobel experimented with different additives. He soon found that mixing nitroglycerin with a type of clay he called *kieselguhr* would turn the liquid into a paste that could be shaped into rods of a size and form suitable for insertion into drilling holes. In 1867 he patented this material under the name of dynamite.

As more tunnels were constructed, the railroad companies began using nitroglycerin, a dangerously volatile liquid explosive.

its way to the Sierra camp, a shipment of it in a San Francisco warehouse killed twelve with such force that inspectors never recovered a single body. Assuming that the explosion was a fluke, the railroad shipped more up to the camp and, only days later, a small amount detonated in No. 6 killing three Chinese and three whites. According to a newspaper report by the *Sacramento Union,* "The construction foreman was blown to pieces, part of him not found."[53]

Fear swept the blasting crews. The few white blasting crews refused to handle the nitroglycerin. The Chinese, however, accepted the challenge and immediately became the next victims of the unpredictable liquid. A pocket of nitroglycerin that had failed to detonate remained in a hole until a worker returning to the tunnel unwittingly struck it with his pick. The blast was so powerful that he was never found. After a number of workers were killed this way, the

Central Pacific abandoned its use, but not the Union Pacific.

Although the deaths were a high price to pay for No. 6, Clement's diligent application of mathematics paid off when all four bores connected. Historian John Hoyt Williams tells the dramatic conclusion of tunnel No. 6 in his book, *A Great and Shining Road: The Epic Story of the Transcontinental Railroad*:

> As Clement finished his measurements and worked out the geometric statistics at a rude desk near the tunnel mouth, he found his most fervent prayers answered. Summit tunnel's four bores fitted together almost perfectly, within a total error in true line of less than two inches. The seemingly impossible had been achieved.[54]

BASKET BLASTERS

Occasionally, the route chosen across the treacherous Sierra mountain range seemed to present insurmountable problems. One three-mile stretch, named Cape Horn by the workers, initially appeared to be impassable. Engineers dismissed blasting a tunnel through the horseshoe-shaped promontory because the mountain was too wide, and they also dismissed carving a straight grade or looping switchbacks because the grade was too steep. Instead, engineers directed workers to cut a roadbed that skirted the outer edge of the mountain. The work was exceptionally dangerous because the sheer drop of one thousand feet from the level of the proposed roadbed would kill anyone who fell.

The Chinese were the only group willing to volunteer for this difficult piece of work that involved digging footholds on the steep slope while trying to drill holes into the mountain for blasting powder. Several fell to their deaths and others were killed by premature explosions when scrambling to get out of the way. After several months, hundreds of barrels of black powder, and several deaths, very little progress had been made.

Hoping to speed up the work and reduce fatalities, a delegation of Chinese approached Strobridge in the summer of 1865 and proposed a solution to the problem. The Chinese pointed out to him that similar problems in China had been overcome by crews using wicker baskets as work platforms hung from the tops of the vertical cliffs by ropes secured above. By using such an ingenious technique, workmen would no longer slide to their deaths, and the holes for explosives could be drilled more quickly. Strobridge ordered reeds to be sent up the mountain.

When the reeds arrived, the Chinese wove them into the baskets and set to work. Adding to the spirit of the adventure, they decorated the baskets

A train is pictured at Cape Horn. Only the Chinese were willing to work on this very dangerous stretch of the railway.

with colorful Chinese characters that gave them the look of Christmas tree ornaments as they precariously dangled in the air. Standing in dozens of tethered baskets, the Chinese drilled holes in the granite mountain face, filled them with black powder, and then lit the fuses. As one foreman witnessed them, "Dangling, they tamped in explosives that had been lowered to them, set and lit the fuses, signaled the men above by jerking a rope, and then scrambled up the lines while gunpowder exploded underneath."[55]

Following a thunderous explosion, the crew operating the ropes would reposition the baskets and the drilling process would begin again.

This new procedure was a success but the crews paid a terrible price. Not all baskets were pulled out of harm's way fast enough, and many Chinese workers along with their baskets were blown up in the process. Records were not kept, but most railroad men believed that the use of the baskets to clear this three-mile-long path around the outer lip of the mountain claimed

❧ PRIDE OF WORKMANSHIP ❧

The Chinese were the only group working for the Central Pacific willing to carve their way through the granite Sierras. It was a point of honor within the Chinese society. Even though the white men working on the railroad resented the presence of the Chinese, they nonetheless respected their willingness to drill and blast their way through the mountains one inch at a time. In spite of the fact that everybody understood the unbelievable difficulty and danger of the work, some railroad executives were always looking for men who could do it faster. This questioning of their superiority was perceived as an insult within the Chinese camp.

Desperate to get the work moving more quickly, Crocker and Strobridge hired a team of miners from Cornwall, England, who were working in California gold mines and had a reputation for being the world's best blasters. Paying them extra wages as well as their transportation to the job site, it was hoped that they would get the tunnels moving more quickly. On February 27, 1877, Crocker testified before a congressional committee about the quality of labor he received from the Chinese. Published in the Report of the Joint Special Committee to Investigate Chinese Immigration, Senate Report No. 689, *Crocker praised the tunnel abilities of the Chinese:*

We went to Virginia City and got some Cornish Miners out of those mines and paid them extra wages. We put them into one side of the shaft, the heading leading from one side, and we had Chinamen on the other side. We measured the work every Sunday morning; and the Chinamen without fail always outmeasured the Cornish miners; that is to say, they would cut more rock in a week than the Cornish miners did, and there it was hard work, steady pounding on the rock, bone-labor. The Chinese were skilled in using the hammer and the drill; and they proved themselves equal to the very best Cornish miners in that work. They are very trusty, they are very intelligent, and they live up to their contracts.

After a few weeks, the Cornish miners were paid off and sent back to the gold mines. Never again did anyone challenge the mastery of the Chinese.

more lives per mile than any other stretch of railroad.

By the time the Central Pacific had completed the first thirty miles over the Sierras, all camp managers recognized the valuable contribution of the Chinese. Their willingness to work with explosives and to do so under the most strenuous conditions prompted many compliments from both Strobridge and Crocker. Nonetheless, the railroad bosses continued to add to the Chinese workers' growing list of dangerous tasks.

SURVIVING IN THE SNOW

Winter added to the already dangerous geography in the Sierras. The summit was only 119 miles from Sacramento, but it would take the railroad camp four years to get there. A key factor in such a slow advance was the winter conditions that regularly scattered dozens of feet of snow across most of the range from September to May.

During the winters the snow-capped Sierras became a death trap to anyone working in one of nature's most unforgiving environments. This was especially true during the 1866–1867 winter, the worst on record, when a series of alpine storms dropped forty feet of snow. Stopping construction during the winter was not an option, and Strobridge insisted that everyone work all twelve months. Complaints and threats of desertion from the crew forced him to change his mind and to furlough the white crew members down to Sacramento for the winter. Most of the Chinese, however, were required to stick with the effort, regardless of the severity of the conditions.

To survive, the Chinese learned to live like moles in a labyrinth of tunnels beneath the snow. This system of tunnels connected their tents, eating places, sleeping burrows, tunnel entrances, and other camp facilities. Although the maze of tunnels demonstrated a brilliant adaptation to adverse conditions, the tunnels provided no protection from avalanches, as historian Stan Steiner indicates in his book, *Fusang: The Chinese Who Built America:*

The Chinese tunnelers were forced to camp, in thin canvas tents, under ten to twenty-foot snow drifts. For month after month, they lived like seals, huddled together in padded cotton clothes. Several of their camps were swept away by avalanches in the arctic oblivion of those mountains, and the dead were not recovered until the snow thawed.[56]

Stories of Chinese killed in avalanches filled local newspapers the entire winter. According to contemporary historian Thomas W. Chinn, "We shall never know the actual death toll that grim winter, but without doubt, loss of life was heavy."[57] In spite of the number of deaths, the railroad foremen pushed the Chinese to keep the work moving forward, even though historian Oscar Lewis believed the railroad company recognized that

[there] was constant danger, for as snows accumulated on the upper ridges, avalanches grew

frequent, their approach heralded only by a brief thunderous roar. A second later, a work crew, a bunkhouse, an entire camp would go hurtling at a dizzy speed down miles of frozen canyon. Not until months later were the bodies recovered; sometimes groups were found with shovels or picks still clutched in their frozen hands.[58]

Without the sacrifices of these winter workers, the owners of the Central Pacific conceded that their part of the transcontinental railroad might never have gotten beyond the 119 miles to the summit. West Evans, one of the white foremen forced to spend the winter supervising the Chinese, declared, "I do not see how we could do the work we have done here had it not been for the Chinamen."[59]

The informality of the railroad's record keeping prevents modern historians from even hazarding a guess at the number who were buried along the route, although scattered references are informative. In 1870, for example, a Sacramento newspaper carried this unsettling report: "A train bearing the accumulated bones of 1,200 Chinese workers on the Central Pacific passed through Sacramento."[60]

Fortunately, not all crews experienced high fatality rates. Two of the crews that worked in relatively safe circumstances and contributed in unusual ways were the logger and bridge crews.

BRIDGE-BUILDING AND LOGGING CREWS

The bridge-building and logging crews were unique because the same men worked on both crews. During the warm weather, the men worked on the bridge crews as the railroad inched up the Sierras, but when the weather turned cold, they put down their hammers and bolts and picked up axes and saws to become the logging crews.

Engineers on both railroads tried to avoid building across rivers and ravines, but both were forced to build many of these massive wood structures, especially the Central Pacific. The two longest and most complicated bridges were the 800-foot Newcastle Bridge and the 1,050-foot Secrettown Bridge that had a curved profile.

Skilled bridge builders understood how to drive pilings stouter than telephone poles and how to cut and crossbrace heavy beams. Such builders were in short supply and were paid handsomely, between $90 and $150 a month, three to four times as much as standard construction workers.

During the winter, crews strapped on snowshoes and headed out into the forests filled with snow to replenish their supplies of timber. Felling large trees was done with double-headed axes and eight-foot-long two-man saws. After the trees were felled and stripped of small limbs, they were dragged by mules or floated down flumes to steam-powered sawmills to be cut into massive beams. To keep production humming, the Central Pa-

cific manned twenty mills full time while pushing across the Sierras.

Not all beams were cut at the mills by machines. Steam-powered mills were new and not always reliable. To back them up, highly skilled lumberjacks remained on the payroll, one of whom reported that they "split their timbers with handheld whipsaws,

Bridge building crews worked on construction in summer and cut wood for the bridges during the winter.

16 by 18 by 20 inches, and from 40 to 60 feet long."[61]

All of the specialty crews on both railroads worked toward the one common goal of preparing the way for the line crews that would set the rails. The work of the foremen, surveyors, engineers, blasters, cowboys, blacksmiths, loggers, and bridge builders all set the stage for the line crew, the crew that mattered most when it came to completing this Herculean job.

LINE CREWS

The line crew was a large, well-coordinated team consisting of between one and two thousand men divided into three distinct subcrews that first cleared the railbed of debris, then performed the final smooth grading, and finally spiked the rails. Skilled railroad building required these three crews to follow each other down the track in a carefully measured, sequential process. Each manual laborer had one specific task to perform such as shoveling dirt, leveling the railbed, running wheelbarrows, swinging twelve-pound sledgehammers, setting dynamite charges, or loading hundreds of steel rails and thousands of hefty wood ties on and off wagons.

First the clearing and grubbing crews removed all boulders, trees, and any other large obstacles from the railbed. Then, directly behind them, the grading crews leveled and smoothed the ground for rail setters who actually spiked the rails to the ties. Maj. Gen. Grenville M. Dodge commented in his book *How We Built the Union Pacific Railway* that "Their force consisted of 100 teams and 1,000 men living at the end of the track in boarding cars and tents, and move forward with it every few days. It was the best organized, best equipped, and best disciplined work force I have ever seen."[62]

Construction superintendents drilled their crews relentlessly at the outset of construction to hone their skills so the path could be cleared, leveled, and the rails set as one fluid process. The Union Pacific learned the importance of precision early on when the first few miles of track went unbelievably slowly; the first mile took eleven days. Within a week or two of practice, however, they were laying track at the rate of a mile per day, and after a month or so they were

From the outset, railroad builders were trained to work with the utmost efficiency.
Here, a well-organized crew lays wood ties.

able to double and occasionally to triple that rate.

GETTING STARTED

The shrill blast of a train whistle at sunrise split the chilly air, signaling the start of the day for the line crews. Within minutes, thousands of scruffy, disheveled men crawled out from under their bedrolls and stumbled out of tents. Pulling on their pants and boots, they scrambled to the nearest stream or water barrel for a quick dousing of cold water.

As the men assembled into their respective teams, each passed by one of the paymasters who counted heads and recorded the names of those who showed up for work, to verify the number who would be paid that day. A second count was made at the noon meal and a third at quitting time. When W.H. Rhodes, a reporter for the *San Francisco Chronicle,* went on an inspection trip of the railroad in September 1868, he asked Crocker about the count and filed this report: "Thus, every morning a count is made of those who go to work, a second of those who eat and a third of those who quit at night. In this way, lengthy bookkeeping is avoided, time is saved, and cheating prevented."[63]

CLEARING AND GRUBBING TEAMS

The clearing and grubbing teams began their day farther from camp than the other two teams that would follow behind. The principal job of the clearing and grubbing teams was to remove all obstacles from the path marked by the survey crews indicating the exact location for the rails. The Central Pacific maintained a significantly larger clearing crew than did the Union Pacific because of the unusually difficult terrain encountered going over the Sierra mountains. Removal of trees and boulders, the most commonly found obstacles, required loading horse-drawn wagons with axes, two-man saws, barrels of black powder, hand drills, and heavy crowbars.

As the crew members made their way up the line, it was their job to clear everything within the markers indicating the rail path. The trees were felled with hand axes and either rolled out of the way or shipped to sawmills. Remaining large stumps had to be ripped from the soil with black powder, a process called grubbing. Some of the stumps were so massive that they required as many as ten barrels of powder to wrench them from the earth. With each explosion, crews had to duck for cover to avoid being hit by chunks of rock and exploding wood.

The most difficult section of road encountered by the grubbers of the Central Pacific was a one-mile stretch at Clipper Gap, high in the Sierras. This stretch required hundreds of barrels of black powder, an amount estimated to have been equal to the powder used by both generals Lee and McClellan at the major Civil War battle of Antietam. Lewis Clement, one of the lead engineers, recalled this stretch saying, "There was snow on the ground probably to a depth of 2 feet and I think that there were over 300 men at work fully ten days clearing off a mile. Those were not Yankee forests [small spindly eastern trees], but forests with trees 4, 6, and 8 feet in diameter."[64]

Boulders were the other major obstruction. The strategies that the clearing crews most often employed were either to roll them out of the way or to explode them into smaller more manageable chunks. Blasting boulders into smaller pieces was the less risky of the two strategies even though it involved powder and fuses. Ideally, the crews would find a large crack in the boulder that could be packed with explosives and ignited. Failing that, they used hand drills to bore a series of holes into which the explosives would then be packed, set with a fuse, and detonated.

Occasionally, large round boulders could be rolled out of the way by harnessing mules to them. This was usually a safe and successful strategy when the road grade was gradual, but tricky on steep slopes. The danger feared by the men was that once a boulder began rolling, the crew might not be able to unharness the mules before they were dragged down the mountain along with it.

The foreman of the clearing crews continually inspected the railbed, barking orders to make certain all large objects were removed, one way or another. When he was satisfied, he hollered out the order for the men to stack their tools in the wagons to move on to the next section.

GRADING

Grading teams, working close behind the clearing and grubbing teams, were responsible for the final smoothing and leveling needed by the rail setters who followed them. As they set out each morning from camp, they harnessed mules to wooden carts loaded with picks, shovels, hundreds of kegs of blasting powder, and a long heavy timber beam called a "drag" that was used in the final smoothing phase.

Grading for the two railroad crews was very different. Much of the route for the Union Pacific across the flat prairie was subject to flooding, requiring many miles of railbed to be elevated at least five feet above the surrounding land. Creating an elevated rail meant hauling in dirt and gravel to build up the railbed, which needed to be at least twelve feet wide for a single track and as wide as thirty feet to accommodate sidings, or sections of parallel track that al-

Clearing and grubbing teams remove impediments such as boulders from a hillside, preparing the site for graders who will level the terrain.

lowed one train to pull over while another passed by in the opposite direction. Sections of track with sidings were called "double tracking" and they were placed at various intervals along the route to accommodate both east and westbound trains.

Where a steep hill lay in the path of the railroad, the crew faced the opposite problem, requiring them to make a cut through the hill to keep the grade as level as possible. To prevent the sides of the cut from collapsing, the graders sliced through the hill from top to bottom forming a cut in the shape of a "V," wider at the top than at the bottom. This process sometimes meant removing thousands of cubic yards of rock and dirt, first by blasting and then by horse-drawn wagons and by hand.

Grading required the most manpower and was considered the hardest work along the construction route, especially in the sweltering summer heat in Nevada, Wyoming, and Utah. The temptation to avoid the exhausting work by hiding from

When faced with a steep hill—the one pictured is sixty-three feet high—graders had to make a deep cut to keep the rail bed level.

the bosses for an hour's nap, shoveling dirt with only half-filled shovels, or feigning an injury was always tempting. Keeping an eye on this sort of loafing, called "haying," was the job of the "walking bosses." According to historian Stephen E. Ambrose in his book *Nothing Like It in the World,* "If a boss caught a man loafing, he cursed at him. The next time, he cursed in a louder voice. The third time the walking boss called the timekeeper and gave the man his time [fired him], adding for the enlightenment of the others, 'This is not a Salvation Army, but a grading outfit.'"[65]

The job of the graders was finished when the foreman completed all of his measurements to ensure it complied with all regulations in the Railroad Act specifying width, slope (if any), curvature (if any), and elevation above flatlands (if applicable). When all measurements complied, he called out the order to move on to the next segment, clearing out for the rail-setting crews to move up.

RAIL SETTING

The rail-setting crew was the last one down the line. This was the crew that made the railroad companies their money, because it was not until the rail setters had completed their work that the federal government handed over their mileage pay.

Rail setters moved down the smoothed railbed with speed and precision. First wood ties, eight by eight inches by eight feet long, were set eighteen inches apart in a straight line, roughly twenty-five hundred to the mile. Just as quickly as the ties were perfectly lined up, the rail handlers followed right behind. At a shout of "up," two three-man teams, working in parallel on each side of the track, picked up two thirty-foot sections of rail with tongs in one synchronized move and at the order "down," dropped them in

৶ MADE IN AMERICA ৳

The Railroad Act of 1862 that authorized the transcontinental railroad was a boon to American travelers, railroad companies, and American industry as well. One of the many clauses in the Act specified that all materials used for construction had to be made in America. Part of the reason for this clause was to announce to England America's economic independence, and the other was to boost American production of iron and steel, the two most important materials used for railroad manufacturing.

All locomotives and the different types of cars, referred to as rolling stock by the railroad companies, were manufactured in one of several East Coast cities. Most of the engines bought by the Central Pacific were manufactured by Roger's Locomotive Works in Paterson, New Jersey, and those for the Union Pacific were made by Norris Locomotive Works in Lancaster, Pennsylvania. All lightweight steel and iron, used for hammers, bolts, fishplates, crowbars, and heavy tools, were also forged in East Coast mills and delivered to the railroad.

The Railroad Act specified all rails be made of iron weighing 522 pounds and were to be twenty-eight feet long, and laid roughly four hundred to the mile. The spikes, also made of iron, had to be driven one per rail per tie, or roughly ten to the rail. Fishplates, the iron plates that connected two rails across the joint, had to be bolted with two bolts, one on each side of the rail. Wood ties, made of American wood (no types were specified) had to average twenty-five hundred to the mile.

Setters knew the basic math of the rails. An average mile required four hundred rails, eight thousand spikes, eight hundred fishplates, and twenty-five hundred ties. Added to these statistics, one that did not involve material was the number of hammer swings to sink a seven-inch spike—three. In rough numbers, the eighteen-hundred-mile transcontinental railroad required 720,000 rails, 14.4 million spikes, 1.4 million fishplates, 4.32 million ties, and 43.2 million hammer swings.

place as close to the gauge of four feet eight and one-half inches as possible. With the rails in place, workers measured the gauge for compliance and adjusted them if necessary. Spikers swinging sledgehammers then moved up to drive the seven-inch-long iron spikes into the wood ties to hold the rails in place. Three swings per spike slammed them into place. A half-inch gap between the rail ends, which allowed for expansion, received a flat piece of iron called a "fishplate" that was bolted across the expansion gap to prevent the rails from pulling apart.

Following the setting of the rails, the supply train drove over the newly laid rails dumping gravel over them as ballast, filling in the spaces between the ties to prevent the rails and ties from shifting under the weight of passing trains. Tampers using heavy pieces of wood posts then pounded on the gravel to make sure that it filled all the spaces between ties all the way to the ground.

The setters had the highest profile of any work gang in the railroad camps. Charles Crocker knew this when he once commented, "Nothing looks to the public as much like making a railroad as the work of laying down the iron on the road bed."[66] Whenever newspapermen came to

Working with remarkable speed and accuracy, a rail-setting crew lays wood ties and rail.

❧ FINAL TRACK TESTING ❧

After the railroad had completed laying the tracks, government commissioners followed on their own train inspecting the track while seated on the cowcatcher of the engine. The government would not pay the railroads for completed track until their inspectors had approved it. The idea was that they would inspect the rails by looking at them and by feeling with their bones whether or not the tracks were straight, level, and in good condition. On the Central Pacific, one government inspector normally stood on the rear platform with binoculars, scanning the rails, ties, gravel, and grade as the train rolled down the tracks. According to John Hoyt Williams in his book A Great and Shining Road, *one such inspector was not as rigorous as the government might have liked:*

[He] laid down, on the front of the car, shut his eyes and composed himself to sleep. The logic employed was that if passengers aboard could sleep, the track must be level and well spiked. The Colonel slept profoundly, and did not awaken until we overtook the end of the road just 307 miles from Sacramento. The Colonel's narcolepsy resulted in another segment of the Central Pacific line gaining approval.

write a great story for their readers back home, the spikers swinging their hammers were the crew members who attracted the most attention. W.H. Rhodes, writing for the *San Francisco Chronicle,* filed this report while in the Sierra Mountains:

> Here we found a very large number of men at work—principally Chinese—laying the track. It would be impossible to describe how rapidly, orderly and perfectly this is done without seeing the operation itself. Vehicles laden with ties are always in advance, and Chinese with gauge and leveling rod place them across the grade, almost as quick as they were placed. The car with the rails is brought up at a gallop and six white men—three at each rail—roll the iron off the car and drop it upon the track with the velocity of steam. The empty car is lifted off the track, and then one fully loaded is drawn to the front, and the same operation repeated *ad infinitum* [forever].[67]

Setting rails straight across the prairie was relatively quick for veteran setters, but setting around a curve was quite another matter. Bending the iron rails was tricky, especially considering that they had to be curved in perfectly matched pairs. Curved rails had to maintain their

❧ THE TEN-MILE DAY ❧

As the sun rose on April 28, the race was on. Chinese workers unloaded sixteen carts of rails, spikes, connecting plates, and wood ties in the first eight minutes. Following the distribution of materials, a team of eight rail setters, four to each 560-pound rail, picked up the two rails with their tongs and dropped them in place. Then the spiking crews nailed the rails in place, straightening crews made sure the rails were parallel and exactly the precise gauge, and finally crushed gravel was tamped in place. The moment the tamping was done, the next load of material was run down the line and the process was repeated.

By midmorning, this assembly line of Central Pacific workers was one thousand men long, setting rails at a record pace of one mile per hour. In the midst of this army of workers, foremen rode back and forth on horseback shouting encouragement while others carried cups of tea to the Chinese workers. By lunchtime the crew had laid six miles of track. Confident of success, the crews took a full hour for their meal.

By dinnertime at 7 P.M., the crews reached just beyond the ten-mile mark. The crews had set roughly 25,000 ties, 4,000 rails, 8,000 fishplates, and 80,000 spikes. Each of the eight rail setters had lifted 124 tons of iron while walking hunched over for ten miles down the track, and each received a bonus equal to four days' wages. Excluding the one-hour lunch break, the crew raced along at the remarkable rate of eighty feet per minute —just under one mile per hour.

The record-setting day involved ideal conditions including the stockpiling of materials along the route the previous night. In any case, the re-

gauge, the precise separation between them, just as on the straight sections. To curve a rail, setters generally placed it over a log or rock and under the keen eye of a supervisor, one or more men would jump on it or beat it with sledgehammers until it achieved the desired curvature.

The ultimate objective of the crews was laying rails as fast as possible. Track-laying competitions to see which railroad company could lay the most miles in one day took place for many months between the crews of the Central Pacific and Union Pacific. Track-laying competitions delighted financiers who knew that they would make sixteen thousand dollars per level mile in addition to 12,800 acres of land.

With each successive competition, the number of miles increased

The crew who laid ten miles of track in one day is pictured here as they near the end of their record-setting labors.

cord was never eclipsed. As noted by a San Francisco reporter quoted in *The First Transcontinental Railroad* by John Debo Galloway:

"It may seem incredible, but nevertheless it is a fact that the whole ten miles of rail were handled and laid down this day by eight white men. These men were Michael Shay, Michael Kennedy, Michael Sullivan, Patrick Joyce, Thomas Dailey, George Wyatt, Edward Kioleen, and Fred McNamara. These eight Irishmen in one day handled more than 3,500 rails."

This newspaper report is significant because it is one of the very rare documents recording the names of common workers. It is equally significant because, with the exception of the eight Irish rail handlers, all other crew members were Chinese and received no recognition.

until one day when the Union Pacific spiked eight miles. Refusing to be outdone, on April 28, 1869, the track-laying competition between the two railroads reached its peak when Crocker wagered and won a ten-thousand-dollar bet that his Central Pacific crew could lay a record-setting ten miles of track in a single day. The crews also appeared to enjoy the competition that included bonuses and an evening meal that was an unusually festive celebration.

Such signs of camp revelry along the otherwise dreary line, however, were actually quite rare. More often than not, undercurrents of dissatisfaction circulated through the camps of both railroads, revealing both subtle and overt friction between the workers and their employers.

CHAPTER 7

CAMP DISSATISFACTION AND UNREST

Problems constructing the transcontinental railroad encompassed more than blasting tunnels through the threatening Sierras or fighting enraged Indians intent on stopping the advance of the Iron Horse. Problems also arose that were internal to both railroad camps.

Most days the construction crews got up in the morning, put on their boots, picked up their tools, and set to work without any unusual concerns or complaints about their jobs. On a few mornings, however, some men did not. Over the course of seven years while pounding out the railroad across America's last remaining wilderness, the men's pay, dangerous working conditions, ill treatment by management, or health fears occasionally prompted them to express resentment by striking or even deserting the railroad.

AN OMINOUS START FOR THE CHINESE

Labor relations between the Chinese and their bosses on the Central Pacific began ominously. Racial and cultural differences between them and white railroad managers became an instantaneous obstacle highlighted by this candid statement by Strobridge during the early days when he refused to hire Chinese workers: "I will not boss Chinese. I will not be responsible for work done on the road by Chinese labor. From what I have seen of them, they're not fit laborers anyway. I don't think they could build a railroad."[68]

Strobridge's concern, which was shared by many Central Pacific foremen, was not entirely a racist point of view. Railroad officials were concerned that the diminutive Chinese, who at the time averaged less than five feet tall with a slight frame, would not be sufficient for setting steel rails and wood ties. Although many railroad men doubted their abilities, Crocker needed men, and as Stephen E. Ambrose points out, he was desperate: "Regardless of the reluctance, Crocker was aware of the labor shortage in California and convinced Strobridge to experiment with a small crew of fifty Chinese, adding rhetorically, 'They built the Great Wall of China didn't they?' "[69]

Crocker's willingness to champion the Chinese resulted in the hiring of thousands more. Both he and

❧ CHINESE HERBAL MEDICINES ❧ COME TO CALIFORNIA

Although the Chinese who worked on the railroad adopted little of the California culture, the reverse was not always true. When the Chinese herbalist Yee Fung Cheung was hired by the Central Pacific to treat sick Chinese workers, the American doctors were amazed at the low incidence of illness among Chinese workers. Although much of the credit for the good health of the Chinese was due to a superior diet and hygiene, compared to that of the white workers, it was clear that diet and hygiene could not explain all of it.

As Yee combed the California hills for herbs to remedy the ills of the Chinese men, he found many that he knew in China and some that were new to him. Following many successful treatments, he acquired an excellent reputation among the railroad men. During the construction of the railroad, Yee continued to operate an herb shop in Sacramento.

While practicing in Sacramento, the wife of Leland H. Stanford, California's governor and one of the four owners of the Central Pacific Railroad, lay dying from a severe pulmonary disorder. After conventional medical treatments failed to restore her health, the Stanfords' Chinese cook located Yee playing a card game at the Wah Hing grocery store. Hearing about Mrs. Stanford's illness, Yee went to his shop and brewed an elixir that ultimately saved her.

The primary herb in the concoction was later identified as majaung, a natural source of ephedrine commonly prescribed by modern internists for pulmonary diseases. Not knowing his real name, the governor's staff called Yee Fung Cheung Dr. Wah Hing after the store he was found in. It was the name that non-Chinese were to call Yee Fung Cheung for the rest of his life.

Strobridge needed workers, but that reality did not create an obligation on their part to treat them as equals to the white worker. Many types of discrimination created a constant source of friction.

Racial slurs and ostracism abounded. The Chinese were derisively called "Crocker's pets" by some and "coolies" by others, an insulting Hindu term meaning unskilled workers. To further insult the Chinese, American historian Stan Steiner explains in his book, *Fusang*, that "the white railroad men wouldn't work within a hundred rods [650 yards] of them."[70] White fellow workers also resented and verbally attacked the Chinese, blaming them for, among other things, low wages. Once when Crocker attempted to explain to white crews that they made more money than the Chinese,

Rail workers lay stone piers for a bridge. The hard working crews expected to be paid regularly and, if they were not, would strike or resort to more violent measures.

one Irishman exploded with this racial slur, "But if it wasn't for them damned nagurs [a racial slur applied to Chinese and blacks] we could get $50 and not do half the work."[71]

A major point of friction that occasionally flared on the worksite was the refusal on the part of Crocker and Strobridge to promote Chinese to positions of authority and greater responsibility. Railroad management steadfastly maintained that only white workers could manage Chinese workers, an attitude that never changed.

TENSION ON THE UNION PACIFIC

Labor relations on the Union Pacific did not include racial tensions because 99 percent of the men were white. Pay, however, was a burning issue from start to finish. Crew members learned that getting their job working on the railroad was often easier than getting paid.

Payday occurred when well-guarded support trains carrying steel safes welded to the frame pulled forward for the dispersal of gold coins. Contacting workers in remote areas far from the main workforce was a bit riskier, according to paymaster W.E. Brown, who recalled carrying the money "on a spring wagon that had guards along with rifles, on horseback."[72]

At no time did the railroad company establish a regular monthly payday; it was simply assumed by all

involved that everyone would eventually get paid. Nonetheless, managers understood that missing a payday by more than a few days was one issue that might push the men to strike.

In May 1869, after missing the payday by more than a week, the tone of the Union Pacific camp became ugly. Major General Dodge dispatched a telegram explaining his concerns about potential unrest: "[I] have been compelled to borrow twenty thousand dollars . . . unpaid men are idle and clamoring for their money."[73] A similar letter was received from head engineer Sam Reed stating, "we must have funds . . . cannot keep men quiet long and damage will be done to the road unless payments are made soon."[74]

The warnings of both Dodge and Reed were correct readings of the dissatisfaction swirling through the camp. Later that same month while the unpaid Union Pacific crew was pushing across Utah, a group of Irish workers, displaying unusual bravado, surrounded the superintendent's railcar and began shouting to be paid. Inside the car along with the superintendent was Thomas C. Durant, one of the directors of the railroad, making an unusual visit. To rescue Durant from the rowdy crowd, a secret hand signal was given to the engineer to pull out of the station at full speed. Before this stratagem could be executed, however, several of the disgruntled employees, armed with pistols, jumped on board. As the train was beginning to pick up speed, one of the armed men ran between the cars and disconnected the superintendent's car from the rest of the train, which continued to speed out of the station.

A handful of gutsy workers held Durant hostage at gunpoint until the railroad company paid up. Following several days of intense negotiations, the railroad realized it was in their interests to send up the paymaster to distribute $235,000 in back pay to the workers in exchange for their agreement to release Durant.

Men called labor strikes for other reasons. A crew of blasters tunneling in Wyoming, who were ordered by the railroad to switch from black powder to nitroglycerin, went on strike because of the increased danger. They were fired on the spot and replaced. While pushing across Wyoming, Union Pacific graders demanded a salary increase from three to four dollars a day. When their demand was rejected, they went on

Thomas Durant (pictured), a director of the Union Pacific, was held hostage for several days by angry workers who had not been paid.

Head engineer Sam Reed refused to negotiate with striking laborers who demanded higher wages for working with nitroglycerin.

strike. The head engineer, Sam Reed, was in no mood to negotiate when he issued this statement: "I have troops to enforce orders and will starve them out unless they go to work."[75] The strikers knew enough about railroad bosses to know they were not bluffing, and they returned to work.

LOW PAY AND DANGEROUS WORKING CONDITIONS FOR THE CHINESE

The most obvious form of discrimination practiced against the Chinese was pay. The Central Pacific refused to pay the Chinese at the same rate as the white workers, even though railroad managers admitted that, as a group, the Chinese were more reliable and more competent than the whites. In 1863 white workers were paid $30 a month plus meals but the Chinese received only $26, excluding meals. Although the Chinese saw wages increase from $26 to $35 over the course of building the railroad, they always lagged behind the whites.

Payment to the Chinese had a very different twist from payment to whites. Not only was the money dispersed differently, but the amount paid was what the railroad believed to be fair for the month, and regardless of accuracy, the amount could not be disputed by the Chinese. In January 1869 a newspaperman who witnessed their payday reported:

> When they [the paymasters] came up to these gangs of Chinamen, the money due them would be already counted out and they would dump the money in one of the Chinese hats for that gang with a statement written in Chinese. There would be no time for explanations. They had to take it whether they liked it or not.[76]

The Chinese never struck over low pay, unfair pay, or late pay. Dangerous working conditions, however, were another matter. During one particularly severe winter storm, Charles Crocker received word that many Chinese workers were about to quit. The winter conditions had cost many men their lives, yet the foremen forced them to continue working in the snow. Historian John Hoyt Williams recorded that Crocker, pompously thinking that the men's spirits might be rejuvenated if they saw him in the snow with them, "personally paid his workers that autumn, dispensing their wages from saddlebags, one bulging with gold coins, the other with silver."[77]

Dispersing gold coins on horseback may have cleverly averted a strike, but the next time it would not be enough. Frustrations again arose within the Chinese camp because they continued to experience far more hardships, suffering, and deaths than any other group on either railroad—a fact no one could dispute. In June 1867 several California newspapers ran stories about a strike by thousands of Chinese blasters, who were refusing to continue their tunnel work because of the dangers and long hours. One day the tunnel workers organized and wrote messages in Chinese characters on placards that expressed their complaints. The workers asked for a raise to forty dollars per month for blasters and a reduction in the length of their workday from twelve hours to ten hours when working outside of tunnels and to eight hours when working inside. As one Chinese spokesman put it, "Eight hours a day good for white men, all the same good for Chinamen."[78]

Strobridge, who early on opposed employing the Chinese, later respected their work habits and readily admitted, "They learn quickly, do not fight, have no strikes that amount to anything, and are very cleanly in their habits."[79] Nonetheless, he had no intention of allowing this situation to continue for fear it would spread to crews beyond the blasters.

Strobridge and Crocker saddled up and rode out to confront the strikers. Both men flew into a homicidal rage, threatening and acting callously toward their men. The Chinese had always feared Strobridge because of his willingness to swing his pick handle at them. According to American historian John Hoyt Williams, "They feared him in their hearts as much as they did the Chinese devil. . . . He had a mild but firm way, which was in the form of a pick handle, in dealing with these fellows."[80] Crocker, equally intimidating at 250 pounds, uncoiled his bullwhip that he nicknamed "Nick." He later admitted to one of the owners of the Central Pacific that he "stopped along the way . . . raising old Nick on the boys . . . everybody was afraid of me."[81]

❧ DISPENSING CAMP JUSTICE ❧

Formal representatives of the law did not accompany the railroad crews down the track. In the absence of sheriffs and judges, construction bosses dispensed whatever justice might be necessary to keep the crews moving toward their objective of setting as many miles of rails as fast as possible. To accomplish this feat, the bosses were recognized by the railroad owners, the military, and the work crews as having the final word in all disputes that might arise within the construction camps, and everyone accepted their autocratic decisions as final—there were no appeals.

The majority of problems that construction bosses had to deal with involved fights resulting from drunkenness, gambling debts, and pressures of hard work under stressful conditions. Sometimes fights escalated from fists to guns, which invariably caused the death of one or more persons. When such things occurred, the construction bosses tended to overlook the causes and consequences so long as the crews quickly returned to work and the incident was forgotten by the crew. Even though one or more men might be dead, the loss was not considered serious to the railroad as long as there were enough workers to keep the tracks on schedule.

When work schedules were impacted by refusals to work, however, the bosses took decisive action. It was not at all unusual for crews to see construction bosses swinging pick handles and shooting at crowds of workers distracted for some reason from their work. Major General Grenville M. Dodge, who worked for the Union Pacific, pointed out in his book, *How We Built the Union Pacific Railway*:

"There was no law in the country, and no court. We kept the peace, and everything went on smoothly and in harmony. Two or three times at the end of our tracks a rough crowd would gather and dispute our authority, but they were soon disposed of."

Yet, when neither pick handle nor bullwhip could resolve the situation, Strobridge and Crocker backed off, realizing that the railroad would be unable to outwait the Chinese. They finally negotiated a compromise, agreeing to an increase of two dollars a month for tunnel blasters' work but nothing more.

WALKING OFF THE JOB

Strikes could be an effective strategy for improving the working conditions and pay for large groups of men will-

It was up to the construction bosses to keep railroad crews like this one on the job.

ing to continue working. Other times, however, individuals or small groups of workers expressed frustrations or resentments to the railroad that management refused to address. In such circumstances, dispirited men simply picked up their bedrolls and walked off the job as soon as the camp was near a town or following payday.

Some men could not tolerate the brutal work pace while others refused to risk their lives for such paltry pay. The initial attraction to the railroad was often the guarantee of steady work, but after a few days or a few months of a relentless schedule, some headed back to the gold and silver mines they had come from. Strobridge once summed up the problem with white workers on the Central Pacific, saying that they were "unsteady men, unreliable. Some of them would stay a few days, and some would not work at all. Some would stay until payday, get a little drunk, and clear out. As usual there is always the lure of the mines."[82]

Illness and injuries prompted many to walk out of camp. Summers in particular took their toll on men who quit either because they had collapsed in the heat or because they saw others collapse. Setting rails across the blistering hot alkali deserts of Nevada and Utah without sufficient water reduced the size of the crews; some died and some took their money and quit. Historian John Hoyt Williams in his book, *A Great and Shining Road,* cites a Central Pacific source that reported temperatures of 120 degrees, "And the men were routinely collapsing and dying on the line from heat stroke and dehydration."[83] According to John Hoyt Williams, Crocker was desperate to keep the men working, and instead of solving the problem with additional water and medical assistance, he tried to solve it with more money. "Crocker authorized hot-season pay raises for all hands."[84]

Injuries had a similar effect. Too many injuries and men limped out of camp with little hope of ever again finding manual work. Although both railroads maintained a small medical staff, injuries such as broken bones, cuts, and lacerations were so common that the railroad did not bother keeping track of them, and the men simply had to endure the debilitating consequences. As historian David Howard Bain reports, "The smaller ones—crushed limbs or lost fingers —were simply recorded; it was becoming either a badge of honor or right of passage for track crewmen to be maimed in such ways."[85]

MASS DESERTION

A man walking off the job was a common occurrence that the railroads could easily handle. Mass desertions, however, caused by a single catastrophic event, could throw the railroads into turmoil. The one

❧ THE TERROR OF CHOLERA ❧

Cholera is an acute, diarrheal illness caused by infection of the intestine with the bacterium *Vibrio cholerae.* During the nineteenth century, before modern medicine and modern sewage and water treatment systems, cholera was feared throughout the country as one of several diseases that claimed the lives of thousands.

At the time of the building of the transcontinental railroad, a cholera epidemic was constantly moving about the country, sporadically infecting communities before moving on. About one in ten infected persons experienced severe symptoms of profuse diarrhea, vomiting, and leg cramps. Of these, two or three, mostly small children and the elderly, experienced a rapid loss of body fluids leading to dehydration, shock, and then death.

The cholera epidemic that ran through the railroad camps was caused by drinking water or eating food contaminated with the cholera bacterium. The disease was especially devastating to the Union Pacific because their water sources as they moved across the dry plains were limited and often of poor quality.

Cholera spreads most rapidly where people are living and working in close proximity, as was the case with railroad workers, and where the corpses of cholera victims were not immediately burned.

Cholera was not easily cured, despite this advertisement's claims.

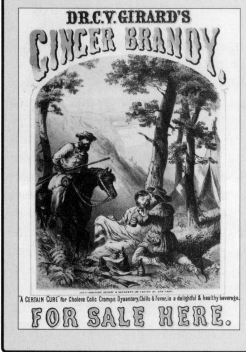

natural catastrophic event most feared was an outbreak of a communicable and incurable disease.

Diseases of various sorts always circulated through both camps, but they were not as common among the Chinese. Some believe it was due to the boiled teas and increased vegetable diets planned by their camp herbalist, Yee Fung Cheung. But in 1868 an epidemic of cholera swept both railroads, claiming many lives and triggering a mass desertion of panicked men rushing to escape the dreaded disease. According to historian John Hoyt Williams, "It struck the Central Pacific's work force, without respect to race. It hit the gangs at the end of the track most severely and the disease for a time greatly reduced the company's manpower where it was most needed."[86]

So many men on the Union Pacific deserted that those who stayed to help the sick and bury the dead were considered heroes. Maj. Gen. Grenville M. Dodge recorded the horror of the disease while praising those willing to put their lives at risk by remaining to help their dead and dying friends: "Every morning those of us who were at the end of the track could see numerous corpses taken out of the working gangs and buried in the dump, and it took a brave, determined man of great moral courage, who is under no obligations, except that of duty, to stay and fight it out."[87]

Desertions were not only linked to the horrors of death. Without a doubt, the most bizarre desertion involved some Chinese crew members who were told by Paiute Indians in Nevada

that they would soon encounter snakes that were not only large enough to swallow Chinese workers but actually preferred eating Chinese over other races. Terrified by what might happen, an estimated five hundred Chinese packed their belongings and returned to Sacramento. When the railroad heard about the incident, they paid men to go on horseback to bring them back, and according to one man witnessing this human roundup, "These men handled these Chinamen like a cowboy would cattle and herded most of them back again. These Chinamen kind of quieted down, and after nothing happened and they never saw any of the snakes, they forgot about them."[88]

As spring weather spread across the Great Plains in 1869, both railroads were in Utah, only a few miles apart. With the end in sight, those still with the railroads looked forward to the joining of the two railroads at Promontory and celebrating the historic event, not backward at the tragedies of the thousands of lost and damaged lives that had been the price of this extraordinary achievement.

An Ending Much Like the Beginning

Both railroads and the United States government chose Promontory, Utah, as the site where the rails would meet. The decision was made to officially complete the railroad with the driving of the last spike on May 10 amid a great celebration that would feature speeches from politicians and railroad owners, men who had rarely, if ever, set foot in the railroad camps.

On May 10 the only symbolic event planned would be the driving of the golden spike by Governor Leland H. Stanford of California, who was also one of the four owners of the Central Pacific. To make this work smoothly, the hole for the gold spike was drilled in the tie ahead of time so the spike would easily drop in.

Exactly at noon, each railroad brought forward an engine so that the two locomotives sat nose to nose. With photographers snapping away to record the epic event, leaders of both railroads made brief speeches and Stanford stepped forward to tap in the gold spike. Not wishing to look like an amateur before his audience, he took a roundhouse swing and missed. Nonetheless, the telegraph operator quickly relayed the message the nation had been awaiting for six years, "DONE." Photographers recorded the scene, and an aide to Governor Stanford grabbed the golden spike and hid it in his railroad car. With much hoopla, all of the dignitaries boarded their private railroad cars and headed home to palatial estates they had built from their profits constructing the transcontinental railroad.

The end had been much like the beginning. Those who financially profited most figured most prominently during the starting ceremonies in Sacramento and Council Bluffs and then six years later at Promontory. Largely overlooked at all of the

A momentous moment is captured in Promontory, Utah. The massive undertaking to join the Union Pacific and Central Pacific railroads is a success.

ceremonies were the crews who did the work.

One or two historic photographs capturing the event in Promontory are found in almost all books documenting the transcontinental railroad. One in particular features the two trains nose to nose, dozens of men leaning from the locomotives, a champagne bottle extended in one man's arm, and in the center, a cluster of well-dressed railroad owners.

What is as remarkable about this photograph as the moment it captured is what it did not. Nowhere in the photograph is a single Chinese worker or white crew member wearing the coveralls or dirty open shirts that identify them as construction men. Most in the photograph are wearing ties, jackets, and hats—unlikely dress for railroad workers in Utah's May sun. Maury Klein, a modern historian specializing in the history of the Union Pacific Railroad aptly noted, as did Henry Morton Stanley one hundred years before him, "No one will know the names of those thousands who provided the brawn, but the greatest accomplishment of all will be theirs: they built the railroad."[89]

NOTES

INTRODUCTION: BUILDERS OF THE TRANSCONTINENTAL RAILROAD

1. Henry Morton Stanley, *My Early Travels and Adventures in America and Asia,* vol. 1. New York: Scribners, 1895, p. 148.

CHAPTER 1: GETTING ORGANIZED

2. Quoted in Stephen E. Ambrose, *Nothing Like It in the World: The Men Who Built the Transcontinental Railroad 1863–1869.* New York: Simon & Schuster, 2000, p. 26.
3. Quoted in Wesley S. Griswold, *A Work of Giants: Building the First Transcontinental Railroad.* New York: McGraw-Hill, 1962, p. 39.
4. Quoted in Dee Brown, *Hear that Lonesome Whistle Blow: Railroads in the West.* New York: Touchstone, 1977, p. 48.
5. Quoted in John Hoyt Williams, *A Great and Shining Road: The Epic Story of the Transcontinental Railroad,* New York: Time Books, 1988, p. 9.
6. David Howard Bain, *Empire Express.* New York: Viking Penguin, 1999, p. 207.
7. Quoted in Griswold, *A Work of Giants,* p. 124.

8. Quoted in Bain, *Empire Express,* p. 232.
9. Grenville M. Dodge, *How We Built the Union Pacific Railway.* Denver, CO: Sage Books, 1965, p. 15.
10. General William J. Palmer, *Report of Surveys Across the Continent.* Philadelphia: W.B. Selheimer, 1869, p. 25.
11. Quoted in Helen Hinckley, *Rails from the West: A Biography of Theodore D. Judah.* San Marino, CA: Golden West Books, 1969, p. 61.
12. Quoted in George Kraus, *High Road to Promontory: Building the Central Pacific (now the Southern Pacific) Across the High Sierra.* Palo Alto: American West, 1969, pp. 130–31.
13. Ambrose, *Nothing Like It in the World,* p. 135.
14. Quoted in Bain, *Empire Express,* p. 301.
15. Quoted in Williams, *A Great and Shining Road,* p. 131.

CHAPTER 2: CAMP LIFE ON THE CENTRAL PACIFIC

16. Quoted in Griswold, *A Work of Giants,* p. 109.
17. Quoted in Griswold, *A Work of Giants,* p. 20.

18. Quoted in Stan Steiner, *Fusang: The Chinese Who Built America.* New York: Harper & Row, 1979, p. 130.
19. *Placerville Herald,* March 17, 1866, p. 7.
20. Quoted in Robert West Howard, *The Great Iron Trail: The Story of the First Transcontinental Railroad.* New York: G.P. Putnam's Sons, 1962, p. 228.
21. Robert F.G. Spier, "Food Habits of Nineteenth Century California Chinese," *California Historical Society Quarterly* 37, no. 2, 1958, p. 133.
22. Quoted in Williams, *A Great and Shining Road,* p. 96.
23. Quoted in Erle Heath, "Trail to Rail," *Southern Pacific Bulletin* vol. 15, chap. 15, 1927, p. 12.
24. Quoted in Spier, "Food Habits of Nineteenth Century California Chinese," p. 132.
25. Howard, *The Great Iron Trail,* p. 228.
26. Howard, *The Great Iron Trail,* p. 228.
27. Quoted in Williams, *A Great and Shining Road,* p. 97.
28. Quoted in Howard, *The Great Iron Trail,* p. 231.
29. Quoted in Griswold, *A Work of Giants,* p. 121.
30. U.S. Senate. "Report Of The Joint Special Committee To Investigate Chinese Immigration." 44th Congress, 2d session, February 27, 1877. Senate Report no. 689, p. 7. Washington, DC. Government Printing Office, 1877.

CHAPTER 3: CAMP LIFE ON THE UNION PACIFIC

31. Quoted in Ambrose, *Nothing Like It in the World,* pp. 217–18.
32. Quoted in Williams, *A Great and Shining Road,* p. 233.
33. Quoted in Kraus, *High Road to Promontory,* p. 258.
34. Quoted in Ambrose, *Nothing Like It in the World,* p. 338.
35. Quoted in Williams, *A Great and Shining Road,* p. 193.
36. Quoted in Williams, *A Great and Shining Road,* p. 126.
37. Quoted in Williams, *A Great and Shining Road,* p. 126.
38. Stanley, *My Early Travels and Adventures in America and Asia,* vol. 1, p. 54.
39. Quoted in Bain, *Empire Express,* p. 380.
40. Stanley, *My Early Travels and Adventures in America and Asia,* vol. 1, p. 157.
41. Dodge, *How We Built the Union Pacific Railway,* p. 119.

CHAPTER 4: SPECIALTY CREWS AND SPECIAL DANGERS ON THE UNION PACIFIC

42. Henry Morton Stanley, *The Autobiography of Sir Henry Morton Stanley.* Boston: Houghton Mifflin, 1909, p. 129.
43. Dodge. *How We Built the Union Pacific Railway,* p. 18.
44. Quoted in Bain, *Empire Express,* p. 354.

45. Quoted in Williams, *A Great and Shining Road,* p. 234.
46. Quoted in Ambrose, *Nothing Like It in the World,* p. 130.
47. Quoted in Ambrose, *Nothing Like It in the World,* p. 208.
48. Quoted in Bain, *Empire Express,* p. 242.
49. *San Francisco Daily Alta California,* June 20, 1868.

CHAPTER 5: SPECIALTY CREWS AND SPECIAL DANGERS ON THE CENTRAL PACIFIC

50. Quoted in Williams, *A Great and Shining Road,* p. 100.
51. Quoted in Kraus, *High Road to Promontory,* p. 151.
52. *Salt Lake City Desert Evening News,* March 25, 1869.
53. *Sacramento Union,* April 18, 1866.
54. Williams, *A Great and Shining Road,* p. 4.
55. Quoted in Williams, *A Great and Shining Road,* p. 114.
56. Steiner, *Fusang,* p. 135.
57. Quoted in Williams, *A Great and Shining Road,* p. 144.
58. Oscar Lewis, *The Big Four: The Story of Huntington, Stanford, Hopkins and Crocker, and of the Building of the Central Pacific.* New York: Alfred A. Knopf, 1941, p. 81.
59. Quoted in Steiner, *Fusang,* p. 128.
60. *Sacramento Reporter,* June 30, 1870.
61. Quoted in Bain, *Empire Express,* p. 363.

CHAPTER 6: LINE CREWS

62. Dodge, *How We Built the Union Pacific Railway,* p. 31.
63. W.H. Rhodes, *San Francisco Chronicle,* September 10, 1868.
64. Quoted in Yen Tzu-Kuei, "Chinese Workers and the First Transcontinental Railroad of the United States of America," doctoral thesis. St. Johns University, New York, 1976, p. 119.
65. Ambrose, *Nothing Like It in the World,* p. 137.
66. Quoted in Griswold, *A Work of Giants,* p. 39.
67. Rhodes, *San Francisco Chronicle.*

CHAPTER 7: CAMP DISSATISFACTION AND UNREST

68. Quoted in Griswold, *A Work of Giants,* p. 110.
69. Quoted in Ambrose, *Nothing Like It in the World,* p. 150.
70. Steiner, *Fusang,* p. 31.
71. Quoted in Griswold, *A Work of Giants,* p. 111.
72. Quoted in Kraus, *High Road to Promontory,* p. 221.
73. Quoted in Williams, *A Great and Shining Road,* p. 272.
74. Quoted in Williams, *A Great and Shining Road,* p. 272.
75. Quoted in Griswold, *A Work of Giants,* p. 269.
76. *Vallejo Evening Chronicle,* January 11, 1869.
77. Williams, *A Great and Shining Road,* p. 142.

78. Quoted in Williams, *A Great and Shining Road,* p. 181.

79. Quoted in John Debo Galloway, *The First Transcontinental Railroad.* New York: Simmons-Boardsman, 1950, p. 144.

80. Williams, *A Great and Shining Road,* p. 134.

81. Quoted in Lewis, *The Big Four,* p. 73.

82. Quoted in Bain, *Empire Express,* p. 208.

83. Williams, *A Great and Shining Road,* p. 208.

84. Williams, *A Great and Shining Road,* p. 208.

85. Bain, *Empire Express,* p. 608.

86. Williams, *A Great and Shining Road,* p. 251.

87. Dodge, *How We Built the Union Pacific Railway,* p. 124.

88. Quoted in Kraus, *High Road to Promontory,* p. 201.

EPILOGUE: AN ENDING MUCH LIKE THE BEGINNING

89. Maury Klein, *Union Pacific, The Birth of a Railroad, 1862–1893.* Garden City, NJ: Doubleday, 1987, p. 36.

BOOKS

Stephen E. Ambrose, *Nothing Like It in the World: The Men Who Built the Transcontinental Railroad 1863–1869.* New York: Simon & Schuster, 2000. This book, tarnished by revelations that the author heavily plagiarized and invented many quotations, continues to have some limited value. The book focuses on the construction of the transcontinental railroad as well as the politics and funding that made it a reality.

David Howard Bain, *Empire Express.* New York: Viking Penguin, 1999. The *Empire Express* is a well-researched, well-written, eight-hundred-page encyclopedia documenting the first three decades of the railroad. It contains many sources overlooked by other historians and includes dozens of well-chosen photographs and topographical maps indispensable to the history of the building of the railroad.

John Debo Galloway, *The First Transcontinental Railroad.* New York: Simmons-Boardsman, 1950. Galloway's book is a wonderful compendium of statistics and quotations that describe the difficulties of building two thousand miles of rail across the western United States. This book provides one of the best technical descriptions of the construction of trestles and roadbeds along the Sierras.

Wesley S. Griswold, *Work of Giants: Building the First Transcontinental Railroad.* New York: McGraw-Hill, 1962. Griswold's work on the transcontinental railroad is focused exclusively on the engineering issues that the Central Pacific and Union Pacific faced as they worked their way across the continent. The book has a good selection of photographs and interesting insights into the major railroad figures.

Robert West Howard, *The Great Iron Trail: The Story of the First Transcontinental Railroad.* New York: G.P. Putnam's Sons, 1962. This is a superb book on the transcontinental railroad written for younger readers. It was used as the basis for a one-hour television documentary for the Public Broadcasting Services. It comprehensively covers the reasons for the railroad, the men instrumental in its construction, and the difficulties completing it.

George Kraus, *High Road to Promontory: Building the Central Pacific (now the Southern Pacific) Across the High Sierra.* Palo Alto, CA: American West, 1969. One of the best books describing the work of the Central Pacific over the Sierras. The story is complete, the style fun to read, and the book has wonderful photographs to elucidate the difficulties of construction over and through the granite mountains.

Marilyn Miller, *The Transcontinental Railroad,* Cincinnati, OH: Silver Burdett, 1986. An excellent easy-to-read book, it is well documented and contains many period photographs.

Henry Morton Stanley, *The Autobiography of Sir Henry Morton Stanley.* Boston: Houghton Mifflin, 1909. Henry Morton Stanley, one of the most famous and flamboyant British explorers of the nineteenth century, begins this autobiography with his difficult childhood. It then describes his adventures running away to sea and becoming a soldier in the American Civil War, watching the railroad being built, traveling to Greece and finally to Africa, where he explored the continent. This book is a compelling self-portrait of the famous adventurer.

———, *My Early Travels and Adventures in America and Asia.* Vol. 1. New York: Scribner, 1895. This is a fascinating account of the life of this famed British traveler. In it, Stanley recounts many of his most memorable experiences traveling in America before and during the building of the transcontinental railroad. Of the many firsthand accounts of the American West during the mid-nineteenth century, this is one of the most intriguing.

John Hoyt Williams, *A Great and Shining Road: The Epic Story of the Transontinental Railroad.* New York: Times Books, 1988. This book has an excellent account of the construction of the transcontinental railroad as well as some of the social problems created by it. Williams exposes the corruption of the railroads, obstacles to the Chinese living in California, and the questionable alliance between the railroads and government.

PERIODICAL

Erle Heath, "From Trail to Rail," *Southern Pacific Bulletin 15,* chap. 15, 1927.

BOOKS

Dee Brown, *Hear that Lonesome Whistle Blow: Railroads in the West.* New York: Touchstone, 1977. Dee Brown's book is a study in the construction of the railroad as well as the corruption that followed. Unlike most books discussing the history of the transcontinental railroad, Brown correctly investigates the impact of the railroad on immigrants, farmers, and other groups that suffered at the hands of the railroads.

Edward S. Barnard, *The Story of the Great American West.* Pleasantville, NY: Reader's Digest Association, 1977. This book covers the American West as it expanded from the Appalachian mountains to the Pacific. It provides excellent artwork and excellent insights into cultural differences of indigenous peoples.

Grenville M. Dodge, *How We Built the Union Pacific Railway.* Denver, CO: Sage Books, 1965. This is an important book because it is one of the very few written by a man who actually managed and planned the railroad. The book primarily discusses issues of interest to managers although it also contains several speeches

Dodge made years after the railroad was finished.

Helen Hinckley, *Rails from the West: A Biography of Theodore D. Judah.* San Marino, CA: Golden West Books, 1969. This biographer of Judah provides a thorough look into his personal life with his wife Anna as well as interesting discussions of his work as reflected in the many letters he wrote to her.

Oscar Lewis, *The Big Four: The Story of Huntington, Stanford, Hopkins and Crocker, and of the Building of the Central Pacific.* New York: Alfred A. Knopf, 1941. Biography of Collis P. Huntington, Leland H. Stanford, Mark Hopkins, and Charles Crocker. Exciting recount of the building of the Central Pacific Railroad.

Maury Klein, *Union Pacific, The Birth of a Railroad, 1862–1893.* Garden City, NJ: Doubleday, 1987. Klein's two-volume work on the Union Pacific presents some fascinating information about the difficulties of building the railroad. The majority of both volumes, however, focuses primarily on financing the railroad and its later corrupt business practices.

General William J. Palmer, *Report of Surveys Across the Continent.* Philadelphia: W.B. Selheimer, 1869. This is a multivolume set of survey reports. Highly technical, it gives insights into the work of the first surveyors and engineers who traversed the Great Plains ahead of the railroads.

Salvadore A. Ramirez, *The Octopus Speaks: The Colton Letters.* Carlsbad, CA: The Tentacled Press, 1982. This book is a collection of letters written by the Big Four of the Central Pacific Railroad during the course of the construction of the transcontinental railroad. Its fascination and value lie with the many comments made regarding questionable business practices in which the four men engaged. These letters, meant to remain private, exist in the public record today as a result of a lawsuit in which they were admitted into evidence. They make for fascinating reading.

Stan Steiner, *Fusang: The Chinese Who Built America.* New York: Harper & Row, 1979. This book is a general study of the Chinese who came to live and work in the United States. It contains one excellent chapter discussing the role of the Chinese building the transcontinental railroad and gives the only Chinese perspective available today.

Yen Tzu-Kuei, "Chinese Workers and the First Transcontinental Railroad of the United States of America," doctoral thesis, St. Johns University, New York, 1976. This is a doctoral thesis that adds little to the significant database of information already available in other major histories.

U.S. Senate. "Report Of The Joint Special Committee To Investigate Chinese Immigration." 44th Congress, 2d session, February 27, 1877. Senate Report no. 689. Washington, DC: Government Printing Office, 1877. This Senate report contains lengthy and detailed testimony investigating whether more Chinese should be allowed to enter the United States. Both Strobridge and Crocker testify on behalf of the Chinese as they answer various questions put to them about the reliability and character of the Chinese who worked on the Union Pacific.

PERIODICALS

Erle Heath, "From Trail to Rail," *Southern Pacific Bulletin* 15, chap. 15, 1927.

E.C. Lockwood, "With the Casement Brothers While Building the Union Pacific," *Union Pacific Magazine,* February, 1938.

W.H. Rhodes, *San Francisco Chronicle,* September 10, 1868.

Sacramento Reporter, June 30, 1870.

Sacramento Union, April 18, 1866.

Salt Lake City Desert Evening News, March 25, 1869.

San Francisco Daily Alta California, June 20, 1868.

San Francisco Evening Bulletin, May 6, 1869.

Robert F.G. Spier, "Food Habits of Nineteenth Century California Chinese,"

California Historical Society Quarterly 37, no. 2, 1958.

Vallejo Evening Chronicle, January 11, 1869.

PICTURE CREDITS

Cover photo: © Bettmann/CORBIS
© Associated Press, Southern Pacific News Bureau, 56
© Bettmann/CORBIS, 11
© CORBIS, 33, 48, 83
Courtesy Central Pacific Railroad Photographic History
    Museum, © 2002, CPRR.org., 19, 29, 30, 61
© Hulton/Archive by Getty Images, 12, 28, 74, 88, 94, 97
Library of Congress, 8, 18, 23, 29, 45, 50, 60, 63, 80
North Wind Picture Archives, 17, 21, 25, 53
© Stock Montage, Inc., 38, 92
Union Pacific Historical Collection, 41, 42, 44, 57, 65, 67,
    71, 77, 78, 86, 89

ABOUT THE AUTHOR

James Barter is the author of more than a dozen nonfiction books
for middle school students. He received his undergraduate degree in
history and classics at the University of California, Berkeley, followed
by graduate studies in ancient history and archaeology at the University of Pennsylvania. Mr. Barter has taught history as well as Latin
and Greek. A Fulbright scholar at the American Academy in Rome,
Mr. Barter worked on archaeological sites in and around the city as
well as on sites in the Naples area. Mr. Barter also has worked and
traveled extensively in Greece. Mr. Barter currently lives in Rancho
Santa Fe, California, with his seventeen-year-old daughter, Kalista.